GP LR

ANGELICA KAUFFMANN

By the same Author

THE FORGOTTEN MASTER: LOUIS SPOHR

THE GREAT REGENT: LOUISE OF SAVOY

THE TRAGIC QUEEN: MARIE ANTOINETTE

Self portrait of Angelica Kauffmann, after the full length picture in the Uffizi Gallery, Florence. Author's collection.

ANGELICA KAUFFMANN, R.A.
1741 – 1807

DOROTHY MOULTON MAYER

COLIN SMYTHE
GERRARDS CROSS 1972

SBN 900675 683

PRODUCED IN GREAT BRITAIN BY
THE GARDEN CITY PRESS LIMITED, PIXMORE AVENUE
LETCHWORTH, HERTFORDSHIRE SG6 1JS

Winckelmann, by contemplation of the ideal works of the ancients, received a sort of inspiration through which he opened a new sense for the study of art. He is to be regarded as one of those who, in the sphere of art, have known how to institute a new organ for the human spirit.

Hegel, from *Lectures on the Philosophy of Art*

Winckelmann, coming in the 18th century, really belongs to an earlier age. By his enthusiasm for the things of the intellect and the imagination for their own sake, by his Hellenism, his lifelong struggle to attain to the Greek spirit, he is in sympathy with the humanists of a previous century. He is the last fruit of the Renaissance, and explains in a striking way its motive and tendencies.

Walter Pater, *The Renaissance*

ILLUSTRATIONS

All pictures are by Angelica Kauffmann unless otherwise stated.

ACKNOWLEDGEMENTS

Before acknowledging all the institutions and individuals who have so kindly given permission and provided illustrations for reproduction in this volume, there are a few people whom I particularly wish to thank: John O'Donovan, who originally suggested the subject of this book; Dr. Monk Gibbon for his advice and constant encouragement; the Earl and Countess of Harewood for the interest they took; the Marchioness of Exeter for the time she took showing me her treasures; Mr. Martin Butlin of the Tate Gallery for his help over the sketch for "The Conjuror"; Andrea Busiri Vici for letting me see many unique documents; Mr. Michael Trinick and Mr. Edward Joy of the National Trust at Saltram and Ickworth respectively, for their kindness and hospitality; James White, Director of the National Gallery of Ireland, for the time he spent with me; Professor Friedlander for his invaluable advice; Sir John Pope-Hennessy for the help he gave me; the Earl and Countess Waldegrave for their assistance; Shane Flynn, who took a great deal of trouble to help me in every way he could; to Anthony M. Clark for allowing me to publish an extract from his penetrating study on Angelica; Professor Zeri for the help he gave me and for showing me his unique documents; and to Professor and Mrs. Gilmartin, Mr. Ronald Freyberger of New York, Mr. Stuart A. Leger, Dr. Oscar Sandner, Dr. Elmar Vonbank, Mr. Denys Sutton, Dr. B. Lohmeyer, Mr. Charles Haughey, Mr. Dennis Mahon, Mr. G. M. V. Winn, Mrs. Donald F. Hyde, Mr. Julian Agnew and Miss Anna Morris for their kindness, enthusiasm and help that they have given me; and the innumerable people both in Ireland and England who kindly showed me their collections but whose pictures I have unfortunately not been able to include.

I wish to acknowledge the kindness of the following individuals and institutions who have allowed me to reproduce pictures and/or photographs in their possession: Editione Alinari; the Antique Company of New York, Inc.; the Bank of Ireland; the Landeshauptstadt and the Vorarlberger Landesmuseum, Bregenz; Mr. Peter Bander; L'Architetto Andrea Busiri Vici; the Museo Capitolino, Rome; Messrs. Christie, Manson & Woods; the Rätische Museum, Chur; the Courtauld Institute of Art; the Marquess of Exeter; the Vorarlberger Handelskammer, Feldkirch; the Freies Deutsches Hochstift, Frankfurter Goethemuseum; Mr. Shane Flynn; Professor and Mrs. T. Gilmartin; The Trustees of the Goodwood Collection; the Earl of Harewood; Mrs. Margarethe Hladik Hämmerle, Dornbirn; The Hyde Collection, Four Oaks Farm, New Jersey; the Tiroler Landesmuseum Ferdinandeum, Innsbruck; the Society of Jesus, Rathfarnham Castle; the Manchester City Art Galleries; the Paul Mellon Centre for Studies in British Art (London)

Ltd.; the Metropolitan Museum of Art, New York; the National Gallery of Ireland, Dublin; the National Portrait Gallery, London; the National Trust at Ickworth and Saltram; the Novosti Press Agency, London; the Art Museum, Princeton University; Protomoteca Capitolina, Rome; the Royal Academy of Art, London; Messrs. Rye, Lawrence & Leman, Golden Square, London; Lord St. Oswald; the Earl Spencer; the Earl of Stair; the Tate Gallery, London; the Uffizi Gallery, Florence; the Earl and Countess Waldegrave; the Washington County Historical Society; the Nationale Forschungs -und Gedenkstätten der klassischen deutschen Literatur, Weimar; R. Winkler, Kilchberg; Professor Federico Zeri; The Victoria & Albert Museum, London; Mrs Joan Cobbe; The Goethe Nationalmuseum, Weimar; and the Kunsthaus, Zürich.

Lastly I wish to thank The Bodley Head for permission to quote from *Angelica Kauffmann, R.A.* by Lady Victoria Manners and Dr. G. C. Williamson, and to Wm. Collins, Sons & Co. Ltd. for permission to quote from *Italian Journey* by J. W. von Goethe, translated by W. H. Auden.

D.M.M.

1

In 1741 a painter called Joseph Johann Kauffmann was living in the town of Chur, in the Swiss Grisons. He was of Tyrolean origin and came from Schwarzenberg, a village in the neighbourhood of Bregenz, but there was very little scope for a painter in such a tiny place, so he had moved to Chur which had pretensions to culture. The town was on the Rhine route north to the Alps, and so was prosperous and well-to-do. From the Eastern Alpine passes travellers followed the river Rhine to Bregenz and then embarked on Lake Constance or took the boat over the Walensee and down the Linth to Lake Zurich. Even under the Romans the town had been important, for the admirable road system which they created followed the lines traced by the pre-Roman Celts. In fact, as far as communications go, Switzerland today is not very different from that of the earliest times; the mountains and rivers have determined the borders of succeeding confederations. As early as A.D. 451, there was a bishopric at Chur, one of the earliest in a country which had been pagan, and through the succeeding centuries the town prospered because of its key position. When Joseph Kauffmann was looking for a more lucrative place to work, Chur was the obvious choice.

When he settled there, the Grisons were enjoying the peace which came at the end of the Thirty Years' War; industries peculiar to Switzerland flourished and travellers were beginning to appear in large numbers. The Arts and Sciences blossomed in a country where religious tolerance had strengthened political diversity. In the last fifty years of the eighteenth century distinguished writers and scientists, from Rousseau and Voltaire to Gibbon and Lavater had made their homes in Switzerland.

Chur was an attractive town surrounded by mountains, and Kauffmann, who was a devout Catholic, felt at home there. The Church, not wealthy enough to be obtrusive, was popular, and the Swiss peasants were not oppressed, as they were in some Cantons, by the pretensions of the nobles who aped the manners of the French nobility. Kauffmann was respected by the local clergy and they gave him profitable commissions. His only sadness was that he had no children. When his wife died, he promptly married again, and on 30 October 1741, his second wife, who had been a Protestant but had become a Catholic when she married, presented him with a daughter. Though he might have hoped for a son, he was delighted with his child and christened her Marie Anne Angelica Catherine—his Angel.

Kauffmann was an unpretentious painter with no aspirations to an exalted position and an honest, frugal man. When Angelica was a year old, he was given some commissions for the church in Monbegna, a town to the South of Chur, and the family moved off to the Valtellina.

By the end of Angelica's second year it was becoming clear to Kauffmann that he had a child prodigy on his hands. Learning her alphabet she took more interest in copying the marginal pictures in the book than in the letters themselves. Whenever she could, the little girl left her toys and grasped her father's pencils and chalks.

Her father had a collection of old prints and these were shown her daily. As she grew older she amused herself by drawing the plaster casts which stood in his studio and reproducing the drawings of the Masters. These she loved, and he would guide her eye and hand until she copied them with astonishing accuracy. A little later in her career, she was to copy many oil paintings—not an ideal education for an artist but the copies were by then being made for financial reasons and for foreign visitors who had commissioned them. She was turning into a lovely young girl. She had dark hair with a glint in it, a bright fresh complexion and brown eyes, sometimes pensive but more often smiling. In addition to teaching her painting, her father gave her poetry and history to read and her mother saw to it that she spoke fluent German and Italian, and some French. Later she learned English, for she had a real talent for languages.

This sort of education did not go unnoticed in a small town: gossips were active, and criticism frequent. Joseph Johann would have been less than human if he had not boasted about his talented small daughter, and people accused him of pushing her too hard. Nobody thought much of his own ability and neighbours resented what they considered his ambitious efforts to win notoriety through his child. But, whatever his personal deficiencies, he knew enough to give Angelica a thorough grounding in drawing, in the value of light and shade and to recognise the work of the great masters when she saw it. Soon she was copying the casts in oil and pastel, never tiring of her life in her father's studio.

In 1752 the family made another move, this time to Como, where better prospects opened for Joseph Johann. Here again, Angelica speedily attracted notice, for by this time she not only painted but was becoming an accomplished little musician with a charming voice. The Bishop of Como, Mgr. Cappucino, heard of her and presently engaged her to paint his portrait, a daunting task for an eleven-year-old, for the Bishop was an eminent and awe-inspiring personage. He was her first patron and professed himself highly satisfied.

Como differed greatly from the simple town where she was born. Instead of the sharp mountain air, to which she was used, there was a languorous climate; and the romantic loveliness of the lake with its changing light and shadow, the oleanders and a thousand other flowers casting their scents on the air, all delighted her and she was to revisit the place towards the end of her life and revive cherished memories. She was flowering into young girlhood, admired, praised, even flattered; and a certain cryptic utterance, made years later, suggests that it may have been here that she first experienced romance. She had only to look in her mirror to see that she possessed grace and charm if not actual beauty. Her voice was developing and she continued her studies so assiduously that by the end of the two years in Como, she had become fluent in four languages, an accomplishment which was to be invaluable to her later on. Her father, more convinced than ever that he had a prodigy on his hands, decided that she was ready for the next step in her education and the family moved to Milan.

Joseph Johann's purpose was not only that his daughter should feast her eyes on the treasures in the galleries, but that she should study them, and this was not easy. Almost no women were allowed to copy in the Milanese galleries, but the persistence of her father managed to achieve it. The legend that she even wore boy's clothes to be unremarked is highly dubious. What is certain is that she was such a skilful student that she attracted the attention of the Governor of Milan, the Duke of Modena, Rinaldo d'Este, who met her, was impressed by her intelligence, charmed by her simplicity, and commissioned her to paint a portrait of the Duchess of Modena. Its success led to recommendations to other distinguished persons and, she was also made free of all the collections in the City. But the first great sorrow of her life was about to overtake her. Her mother died, a shattering blow to both Joseph Johann and Angelica. This quiet woman, in an unobtrusive way, had kept the ambition of father and daughter within bounds, had given Angelica a deeply religious upbringing and had always been sparing with flattery, whereas Joseph Johann had been so overwhelmed by this young creature, compact of all the talents, whom he had produced, that he gave in to all his daughter's whims, feasted on her success and enjoyed with her the revenue which it brought to the rather meagre family purse. It was probably the loss of his wife which drove Kauffmann now back to his birthplace, the village of Schwarzenberg, encouraged by a commission to decorate the church in his old home, for which he had been recommended by Cardinal Pozzobonelli to Cardinal Roth, the Bishop of Constance.

Schwarzenberg, a small village deep in the Bregenz Forest, is little changed from what it was in Angelica's time. Today it has a road. In 1757 it was reached along narrow pathways, over rocky streams, and up and down steep hillocks. One came to the comfortable homes of farmers and peasants inhabiting their steep roofed chalets, heard the sound of cowbells, the shouts of children, and the church bell calling to worship in the large church with its carved wooden pillars. The church's door opened on a magnificent view over mountain and valley, and through it came the smell of pine and oak and fertile earth, of baking and brewing, with a spirit of friendliness and calm brooding over all.

It was a startling change from the princely society in Milan. They lodged with Kauffmann's brother. Opperman says that the goatherd's cottage and the homely fare offended both Angelica's nostrils and her palate, and it was not until she had passed some time there, and found a friend in the person of the parish priest, that she began to feel at home. He made her see things differently and she willingly rose at daybreak to wade through the snow or rain to Mass, for her home was at some distance from the church. In later years she often spoke of this, and her piety throughout all the vicissitudes of her life was one of her most marked characteristics.

The decorations which she and her father had executed in the church pleased the Cardinal Bishop so much that he commissioned other works for his own house in Morsburg, and recommended them to his friends. Moreover he sat to Angelica for his portrait, which she finished in Constance; for father and daughter were once more on their travels. Angelica's restless spirit had wearied of the quiet life, and the painter thought it time that she should continue her studies. So they slowly made their way in the direction of Italy, stopping for a time at the residence of the Count de Montfort in order to paint the portraits of the noble family. And here Angelica made the first decision in her life. All her biographers agree that she was a young woman of remarkable charm; although her beauty was not regular, her expression of tender sweetness and amiability made up for any classical deficiency. She was exceedingly graceful, and nature as well as the company she met in noble houses had taught her to bear herself with elegance. Also by now she possessed a singing voice far above that of an amateur. In short she was in many ways an astonishingly accomplished and desirable young woman.

So thought a young musician then resident in the Count's house. It is just possible that he is the anonymous admirer hinted at by Opperman and who, he maintains, would have been most likely to make her happy. She found it hard to choose between his love for her, coupled with his insistence that she should forsake painting and take up an operatic career, the vocation which hitherto she had always had in mind. The glamour of the stage tempted her, the applause of the public seemed far more exciting than the endless work at a picture, and at her elbow was her father who relished the idea of the quick return which the stage would bring. Love, romance, wealth and applause, all spoke to the young Angelica. But once more destiny intervened in the shape of a wise old priest. He knew that both the Kauffmanns were devout Catholics, and as such he represented the difficulties the girl would encounter in an actress's life; the temptations, the spiritual insecurity, the really unprincipled surroundings of the theatrical world. In this way he gained his point. Angelica decided to continue her artistic life. Later she commemorated this crisis in a picture, "A Female Figure allured by Music and Painting", produced in 1760. And, according to a story told by Zucchi[1] to Rossi,[2] she depicted the young musician as the poet in her "Orpheus and Eurydice" one of the many prints made from her work which is to be found in the British Museum.

[1] Her second husband.
[2] Her first biographer.

Johann Joachim Winkelmann. Courtesy of the Kunsthaus, Zürich.

2

Turning their backs on the rejected suitor, father and daughter made their way to Parma where she had an opportunity of diligently studying the paintings of Correggio. One may trace in much of her later work the influence of his use of chiaroscuro, his sweetness and the flowing beauty of his form. From there to Bologna was but a short journey and the great school of the Carracci and Guido Reni was her good father's objective. He knew the glory of Annibale Carracci's drawing and once in the town he became aware of the fabulous collection of Guercino's drawings, recently discovered. Amongst all these splendours Angelica could work to her heart's content. It seems likely that visits were also paid to Cremona and Piacenza for all these towns lie so close together, and all contain masterpieces of art.

By easy stages they came at last to Florence in June 1762. Here she at once encountered considerable opposition from the other artists working in the galleries, who resented the advent of a woman, and especially a young and good-looking one. Why was she not staying where she belonged, in some man's home caring for him and his children? But by her own perseverance and her father's stubborn support, and aided by the introductions they brought with them, she finally succeeded in finding a room to herself in what is now the Uffizi. There she worked from morn to night, copying, drawing in chalk or pencil, and by dint of selling some of these copies earned enough to keep them, although poorly. By the time she arrived in Rome in January 1763 she was sufficiently well known for a note to appear in a contemporary catalogue: "Miss Angelica Coffman (?) arrived in Rome from Florence 1763." She had reached the centre of artistic influence.

Rome, the Mecca of all artists both then and now, was at this period socially at its most brilliant. Although the State was always short of money, the nobility kept up a superficial splendour, lavishing money on equipages and hordes of servants, while the poor could always depend on charity from the Vatican. So active was the charity that any beggar in his rags could be sure of the price of a meal from a passing stranger, and he accepted it as his due, for was not generosity enjoined by God? Prostitutes, that necessary evil, were sheltered in homes, orphans were cared for in twenty hospices, the girls received a dowry when they left. There were no proper roads and the streets and lanes were littered with rubbish and ordure. But though they were uncomfortable, the Romans were extraordinarily healthy and what was just as noticeable, gay laughing people, always ready for a joke or a song. So that when Angelica and her father took up their lodging they found none of the well-to-do bourgeoisie they had been used to in the Grisons or even in Milan, but a society divided into an estimated 70,000 who did absolutely nothing and a nobility who existed for pleasure and show of one sort or another. Apart from both these, but partially dependent on the latter, were the artists. Over all brooded the languid *dolce far niente* encouraged by the necessity for the daily siesta in the torrid heat of summer.

The Kauffmanns were well received in the artistic world and were fortunate in making the acquaintance of the wife of the artist Raphael Mengs, who as a peasant girl had sat to him as a model and who now was a beautiful creature, voluptuous and essentially kindly at heart. Theirs was a romantic story. He had been sent back to Rome from Dresden to paint a "Holy Family" for Augustus III. One day in the street, he passed this lovely young creature and exclaimed instantly, "*Ecco la Madonna che tanto cerco!*"[1] She, eighteen-year-old Margaretta Guazzi, had not lost her homeland, but Mengs had found his. They remained in Rome, widely popular; and Winckelmann could write to a friend after his arrival in the city, "Without Mengs, I would have been as in a desert here. I spend most of my

[1] "Look! the very Madonna that I've been in search of."

Bacchus and Ariadne. Courtesy of the Landeshaupstadt, Bregenz.

evenings with him." The artist himself was absent from the city when Angelica arrived, but through the well-disposed Margaretta the Kauffmanns were introduced to the great Winckelmann, and in him she found her first real genius, whose teaching was to colour her thought and art for the rest of her life.

In 1741 it was a good moment for any artist to be in Rome. The excavations at Herculaneum had begun; it was too soon for the full impact of Graeco-Roman art to have effect, but under the influence of Charles III of Naples the discovery of Pompeii made a further and far more considerable disclosure. There had begun the reaction in Italy against the High Baroque, and Rome was ripe for the development of neo-classicism. The twisted convoluted forms, the play of light and shade on polished or rough surfaces resulted in a kind of frenzy of movement which leaked over into sound, thus trespassing on the borderlines of each art. In "The Rape of Proserpina" by Bernini, the maiden shrieks, the god shouts, the leaping dogs howl, and confronted by the immense calm of the classical figure, or the wordless control of the Dying Gaul, it is easy to understand the revolution in artistic thought which was taking place.

If the "renaissance" which Winckelmann helped so much to bring about was a genuine one, we will, freed of our prejudices, be able to see in the near future[1] the very considerable achievement of artists like Mengs and Tischbein, Angelica Kauffmann, Gavin Hamilton, James Barry and West in the field that they had been encouraged to follow. Amongst these half-forgotten names, Angelica's has survived. Though tinged with a faintly sentimental taste, her classical compositions show a softer outline, a less economical use of detail. She participates in the terror of the forsaken Ariadne, the desolation of the despairing Andromache. They are less statuesque and more womanly.

J. J. Winckelmann had been a poor German schoolmaster, teaching himself Greek and Latin in his obscure village, but he had the good fortune to find a blind rector

[1] An Exhibition.

whose reader he became, and who gave him the run of a not unworthy library, where he could study to his heart's content. Then, after a brief stay in Berlin, he had gone to Hallé and met the man who definitely set the course of his life. After putting the great Ludovische library in order he had travelled to Dresden to become librarian to Count Bernard where his first literary efforts appeared in a restrained style well in keeping with his passion for Purity in Art.

And then, soon after he had completed his *History of the Arts* in 1755, he scraped together his small savings and with his pension of two hundred thalers he set out for Rome. Here he was to achieve a status of an almost unique kind, and by his writing and teaching to revolutionise taste. Here, as Goethe has written, "He saw his wishes fulfilled, his happiness, all his hope satisfied. His ideas stood in reality before him; and with wonder he wandered through the remains of a gigantic period. He could lift his eyes to them as easily as to the stars and every hidden treasure opened itself for him at the cost of a few pence." He could feel in its full force what the Greeks had felt when every high aspiration of man was enshrined in art, so that they could say "That he who had not seen the OLYMPIC Jupiter had not lived". He had the good fortune to find almost at once a wealthy and influential patron, the Cardinal Albani, who put him in charge of the marvellous collection of classical art which he had been able to assemble in his palace.

This was the teacher to whom the young, ardent and impressionable Angelica listened, and with whom she worked. He spoke of the unity of Truth and Beauty, he urged that the representation of beauty should be the highest aim of the artist and that, of all beautiful objects, the human form in its perfection was the most divine. But he also set rules for the artist to follow in such delineation, and for these the study of Greek art seemed to him of pre-eminent importance. The Greeks could see daily the lovely bodies of the youths and maidens as they ran and wrestled in the gymnasia in the sunshine, and could for-mulate their notions of proportion, balance, motion and

repose. Beauty, said Winckelmann, is one of the great
mysteries of nature, and the delineation of the nude figure is
grounded on the knowledge of measure and proportion.
The beauty of the nude in sculpture was axiomatic with
him. He likened the forms of beautiful youth to the purity
of the surface of the sea, simple-seeming yet ever changing, the lines flowing imperceptibly into one another.
Colour can assist beauty, it heightens the form but it does
not constitute it. This must have sounded strange to
Angelica, who had immersed herself in the colour of
Caravaggio and Guido Reni. Moreover she could not
follow her prophet into the study of the nude model, this
being prohibited for women, but she could see in some of
Rome's palaces and museums the marvellous works of art
which Winckelmann's Greeks had produced. Here again
his teaching helped her but also hindered her. Coleridge
speaks somewhere with scorn of "poems distilled from
poems". But paintings distilled from paintings are nearly
as dangerous an objective. Nor is moral idealism ever a
sufficient substitute for aesthetic conviction. Although
Greek art occasionally seems to justify a sculptor in
representing young heroes with such a conformation of
face as to leave their sex doubtful, it is a dangerous
precedent. Purity, simplicity, dignity, loftiness and serenity
can be characteristics of manly beauty, and certainly when
we look at the Apollo Belvedere, there is little to choose
between this glorious triumphant face and that of the
archaic Greek statue of a woman. Angelica could contrast
the ineffable calm of this work with the contorted, convul-
sive movement of a Bernini masterpiece, and she may have
heard the story of the workmen in the temple of Apollo
who, seeing Theseus passing, took him for a lovely virgin
because he was dressed in a long robe and were astonished
to find he was a man going into the city unattended,
which, according to the custom of the day, no young
woman could do. Winckelmann deprecated excess in all
the passions. It must be rigorously excluded and he in-
stanced the representation of Hecuba on the relief in
Grotta Ferrata where her head is bowed down and her

right hand is pressed upon her forehead in token of the fullness of her sorrow, yet she sheds not a tear sitting by the body of her dead son Hector. Grief there is choked by despair. In Angelica's later work, we shall see again and again the indirect fruit of this teaching: in her "Abelard's Farewell to Heloise", or in "Hector's Farewell to Andromache" the same noble restraint is evident.

Winckelmann was to die in the most tragic fashion, betrayed by his very love of the beautiful. On a return journey from Vienna to Italy, he was indiscreet enough to show some very lovely gold Greek coins to someone in the inn, where he had taken refuge, and was murdered for the sake of them that same night. Long before that, however, he had become what might almost be called the artistic dictator of a whole generation. In Germany his rulings were accepted almost as sacred writ. And in England he had considerable influence largely through Angelica and West.

Angelica was delighted to meet her new celebrity, and as for the great teacher, he was enchanted with his young student. He wrote to a friend: "My portrait is being painted by a rare person . . . she is very proficient in oil portraits. My own, which has cost thirty sequins, is quarto size. The young woman I am talking of was born at Costuiz (others say at Chur), and was brought to Italy by her father, who is also a painter. She speaks German just as if she was a Saxon, also Italian, French and English; therefore, every Englishman who comes to Rome wants his portrait taken by Angelica. I think she can be considered a beauty, and as far as singing is concerned, she ranks with our best *virtuosi*. Her name is Angelica Kauffmann."

Winckelmann's praise brings us to the difficult task of assessing Angelica's actual appearance. It is always interesting to try and build up a visual image of someone whom we shall never see but for whom there is an abundance of pictorial evidence, the signed and attested statements of witnesses who have made affidavits since they cannot be present at the trial. Not many painters' works can be accepted as sworn testimony. There are great portraits which are bad likenesses and good likenesses which are highly-indifferent portraits. In the case of Angelica there is almost a plethora of self-portraits, as well as a number of delineations by highly accomplished artists, such as Reynolds, Dance, Edridge and others. And there is a fine bust in the Protomoteco Capitolina, Rome, done, possibly posthumously, by her cousin Johann Peter Kauffmann (1764–1829). The self-portraits vary from the pensive, painted for the Artists' Gallery at the Uffizi, to the down-right plain one in the dress of her mountain canton, which was reproduced eighty years ago as the frontispiece to Frances Gerard's biography and in which Angelica has made herself look like a hatted Swiss farmgirl. She gazes out on the world with dour contempt and there is none of that sweetness of disposition which we know for a certainty that she possessed. A much more idealised peasant-Angelica, holding a basket of flowers, figures in the admirable oil painting and preliminary sketch which passed into the possession of the Duke of Rutland. Reynolds' portrait makes her serious almost to the point of school-marmdom. But we know from an abundance of sources that she could be gracious and lively. She was not dramatically beautiful or startlingly distinctive. Her face does not suggest sensuality but it does suggest intelligence and human interest and very real charm. It is quite easy to believe that she made a number of superficial conquests as well as having her ardent admirers of both sexes. Her nose seems to have been longer than the average and thickened at the end which gives it an upturned look; her eyes thoughtful; her mouth wide and sympathetic. The general consensus of opinion would seem to be that she had beauty and animation in youth and that she retained her personal charm to the very end of her life. Goethe's and Herder's rhapsodies could hardly have been possible if by then she had been a worn-out disappointed woman. The painter who has been most severe to her is Edridge, who has given her such a mop of jet black hair in tight curls that it almost suggests a West Indian rather than a mid-European origin for her. Dance, who was deeply enamoured of her, has, in a delightful painting now in the National Gallery of Scotland, contradicted most of his fellow-artists by giving her a slightly upturned, indeed almost retroussé, nose in startling contrast to her own version under the farm-maiden's straw hat, and indeed to all the self-portraits. He does the same, much more unkindly, in a drawing of her with Sir Joshua Reynolds— his hand raised to his ear as though to catch what she is saying—which is to be found at Harewood House. But then Reynolds was rumoured to be his supplanter. What we can take as generally established is that Angelica's physiognomy was in its own way nearly as charming and pre-possessing as her disposition, as to the amiability of which there is hardly a dissenting voice, but that it was a gentle almost subdued type of charm rather than a striking one, a charm eminently suited—though not altogether fortunately so—to many of her less vital classical recreations in which she herself figures. Rossi says of her, "There was a witchery in her sweet blue eyes, and in the pupil so much expression that one could almost guess her thoughts before she spoke."

3

The portrait of Winckelmann is a very fine piece of work and fully deserved all the praise which it received. It is endorsed as a likeness by the painting which Mengs made of him. It must be remembered that all this time Angelica was the breadwinner, so when she received a commission to make copies of some pictures in Naples she was glad to accept; she may also have felt curious to see this far-famed and beautiful city. The reality must have surprised her. The beauty was there, the wonderful bay, with its forest-clad shores stretching into the distances of Posilipo and Sorrento, the terrifying mountain, always potentially threatening, the overwhelming palaces; but also the dirt, the superstition, the hordes of idle *lazzeroni*, all these must have disturbed the tidy Swiss minds of Joseph Johann and his daughter.

However, their stay was short and lucrative, and they returned to Rome with their exchequer replenished in April 1764, and Angelica at once took up her half-finished portrait of Winckelmann, one of the best she ever painted.

She now applied herself to the study of architecture and perspective, and since her father was ill-fitted to instruct her, it is highly probable that she worked with Piranesi and Clerisseau, both of whom were active in Rome at that time. But she also steeped herself in the literature which was so fashionable, and for her so important, for she needed the fables and great myths as subjects for the classical pictures which were becoming the rage. It was no wonder that foreigners from every country crowded into Rome at this time. The many Galleries were full of the treasures unearthed by the archaeological researches which had proliferated since the beginning of the century. At first excavations were conducted in a disastrously haphazard fashion.

Now through the discovery of the city plan, engraved in the reign of Septimus Severus when the Empire was at its height, a lead was found. And the accession of Charles III of Naples, who brought his Farnese treasures to that city, gave archaeology a more directed turn. The influence of the art and literature-loving Pope Benedict XIV also helped, as did his founding of the Academy of History and Roman Art.

Since by this time Angelica could speak English fluently, it was from travellers from that country that she received her most frequent and best paid commissions. Every young gentleman making the Grand Tour, which was to finish his education, wished to take home with him some memento of his stay in Italy; but here too Angelica found competition, for English painters were numerous in the city. Eminent in their ranks were Gavin Hamilton, who was an influence in her work, and Dance, who became important in her life for other reasons.

Rome seemed to be giving her everything she needed. She won all hearts by her youth and her enthusiasm. It may have been her intention to please but it came naturally to her. One does not need to be a coquette to make men unhappy. One fellow-artist she did unquestionably make unhappy and there is a certain mystery attached to her behaviour to him which could possibly account for the accusations of coquetry which have sometimes been made against her. He was Nathaniel Dance—"as honest a man as there is in the world and had very strong affections", as his own brother described him—who took the name of Nathaniel Holland when he was later made a baronet. Farington in his Diary tells us the story. "George Dance," he says, "went to Italy by sea. He sailed from Gravesend in December 1758 and did not arrive in Rome till the end of May following— having had a tedious passage and stopping at Florence where his brother N. Dance met him. N. Dance (now Sir Holland) went to Italy in 1755, having before that period been about two years as a pupil with Hayman, where he became acquainted with Gainsborough. In Rome he became acquainted with Angelica Kauffmann and was so enamoured of her, she encouraging his passion, that when he came to England, whither she had also come, it was settled between them that they should marry. But in England she became acquainted with Sir Joshua Reynolds, who showed her much attention and it is supposed she looked to him hoping he would offer Himself to Her. Her reception of Dance having become more cold, and her intercourse with Sir Joshua being noticed by him, he remonstrated with her in such a manner that she complained of his temper and assigned that as a reason for now refusing to marry him. His passion for her was extreme and he engaged her father to write to her, but all would not do, her resolution remained unaltered. Dance said she never was beautiful, but there was something amiable and feminine in Her appearance that engaged people to Her."

So all this was mere hearsay,[1] and hearsay given rather late in the day. It is an instance of hindsight and will be better considered in its later and proper context when we come to see Angelica in London, admired by one of the greatest authorities on Art, as well as the numbers of English artists in that city, feeling her way into ever greater mastery of her own art. It could easily have meant less to her then to be desired by a man who had a position of some wealth in his own country, was a good painter, and had an attractive personality. The contract made between them in Italy, if there ever was one, was not firm, but it may have been sufficiently satisfactory to Dance to make him think that, when she arrived in England, he had sufficient reason to expect her to keep it.

It is probably utterly wrong to see her merely as a spoilt and capricious young lady. One can look at it another way. Here was an artist deeply involved in her growing powers, stimulated by the inspired teaching of a genius, feeling within herself the possibility of attaining, if not perfection, at all events a reputable status among her peers and yet tempted, because she was a woman, by the proffered love of not unimportant men. Perhaps, too, she was a little tired of

[1] Farington's diaries were written between 1793 and his death in 1821 so that any comment on Angelica's life was mainly obtained through gossip.

the constant need to earn for herself and her father the
necessary funds for their mere existence. The way ahead
looked hard and long, and the offered ease was close at
hand. Not even Farington suggests that she engaged
herself definitely to Dance in Italy. Nor do we know what
part Joseph Johann played in all this. It would seem
probable that he urged her to wait; she was young and only
at the beginning of her career. Should all the hard work go
for nothing? In any case, nothing was settled, and Dance
was left to hope.

It was not merely in the various princely galleries that
artists found inspiration. At least as exciting were the ruins
with which Rome was full. Piranesi immortalised the wild
beauty of these monuments to ancient history. The work of
tidying up and developing had hardly begun, and to stand
where Caesar stood and was murdered, to feel the great past
sweep over one, was only made more poignant by the
picturesque confusion of flower and bush which partly hid
pillar and wall. One of Goethe's friends wrote to him,
"It would be a mistake to wish that one had been a
citizen of Athens or Rome. Only from a distance, far
removed from all meanness, only as the past should
antiquity be viewed ... I can imagine for myself two
dreadful things; if the Roman Campagna should be built
over, and if Rome became a police town in which no one
carried a knife any longer. If a really orderly Pope arrived,
which may the Cardinals forever forbid, I shall leave. Only
while Rome possesses such a noble anarchy and while
Rome is surrounded by such a heavenly wilderness will
there be room for the shadows, of whom one is worth more
than a whole generation."

This was the Rome which Angelica saw when she
strayed through it with her ears ringing with
Winckelmann's inspired words; when she and her father
could sit over a simple meal in the open air with her artist
colleagues talking, talking, with the Roman sky above them
and water from some fountain tinkling close by; or when, as
no doubt she must have done, she could stand beside
Winckelmann himself before the statue of the great Apollo

and hear his impassioned words describe what he considered the greatest work of art from antiquity. These were magical days and months for the young painter, and when she could add the praise which came to her so freely and be charmed and flattered by the numerous devotions she inspired, she may be forgiven for getting a little "above herself". J. T. Smith, all too prone to gossip in his life of Nollekins, tells a malicious story of how when "she was at Rome previously to her marriage she was ridiculously fond of displaying her person and being admired, for which purpose she one evening took her station in one of the most conspicuous boxes of the Theatre accompanied by Nathaniel Dance and another artist, both of whom, as well as many others were desperately enamoured of her. Angelica perhaps, might have recollected the remonstrance of Mrs. Peachum, where she says:

'Oh Polly, you might have toyed and kissed,
By keeping men off you keep them on.'

However, while she was standing between her two beaux, and finding an arm of each most lovingly embracing her waist, she contrived, whilst her arms were folded before her on the front of the box over which she was leaning, to squeeze the hand of both, so that each lover concluded himself beyond all doubt the man of her choice."

This may or may not be true, but to conclude from it that Angelica was already an accomplished flirt, as some of her biographers have done, seems a little harsh. That she was capable of flirtation is perfectly possible. She may even have told this story against herself. She was twenty-three, intoxicated by the atmosphere of the city where she found herself, and probably glorying in her own power as young women will. But she never averted her eye from her ultimate purpose, to paint, and to paint as well as it was in her power to do.

The portrait which she painted of Winckelmann has been acclaimed the finest she ever produced. This is an exaggeration. In her portraits of men—which most certainly are quite the equal of those of women—not a trace of

the feminine quality of her classical pictures exists. Over
and over again, one feels that the intellectual stature of the
sitter has been conveyed and as an instance of this one has
only to look at the portrait of the eminent Dr. Tissot, the
friend of Voltaire. Her artistic reputation might be higher
today if she had kept to this one branch of painting. She
had the inestimable gift of seizing the likeness of her sitters
not in a photographic sense but as an indication of their inner
characteristics. Hence the flattering nickname bestowed on
her by the Germans, "*die Seelen Mahlerin*"—"the Paintress
of the Soul". The secret of her success with innumerable
clients was partly her own sympathetic nature. One can
only find two who have left a record of dissatisfaction,
Goethe and the Grand Duchess Amalia, and it is difficult to
understand why Goethe was dissatisfied. Had she not
dramatised him sufficiently, in the manner of Tischbein?

While English writers and critics tend to lean towards a
cynical view of her character at this time, the Germans love
to describe her as "a shy dove". She appeared to them as an
unspotted young girl, a "sacrificial lamb of art", as Herder
later described her. Despite her success in that branch of
art, Angelica's intention was not to make portrait painting
her chief career. She aspired to be an allegorical and
historical painter, and Rome's mood of archaeological
enthusiasm, and all that she saw and heard, contributed to
this plan. She was gradually evolving a style not entirely
peculiar to herself, for Batoni, Mengs, Vien, Langrance, and
others, all employed it, but one in which she was considered
particularly successful. Even in her own time however there
were dissenting voices—for example, Dr. Johnson's pun-
gent, "I had rather see the portrait of a dog that I know
than all the allegorical paintings they can shew me in the
world".

4

In July 1765, Joseph Johann and his daughter left Rome and proceeded to Bologna. Their stay was short for in October they arrived in Venice. It is likely that Angelica's fame had preceded them, for she seems to have made acquaintances among the artists and visitors very quickly. There is no record of their stay in Venice, which lasted a little less than a year, though it may be assumed that they went there in order that she might study the colour of the great masters. It is not difficult to imagine what this ardent student felt when she first saw the works of Titian, Tintoretto and Paolo Veronese. But first the city itself, bathed in its ever varying translucent light, must have affected her much as it affected Ruskin when he stood for the first time between the narrow pillars of the opening into the Piazza and could write, "Between these pillars there opens a great light, and, in the midst of it, as we advance slowly, the vast tower of St. Mark seems to lift itself visibly forth from the level field of chequered stones; while on each side the countless arches prolong themselves into ranged symmetry, as if the ragged and irregular houses that pressed together in the dark alley had been struck into sudden obedience and lovely order." He goes on to speak of "a multitude of pillars and white domes, clustered into a long low pyramid of coloured light . . . five great vaulted arches, ceiled with fair mosaic and beset with sculpture of alabaster, clear as amber and delicate as ivory, fantastic and involved, of pale palm leaves and lilies and grapes and pomegranates and birds . . . and in the midst of it the solemn forms of angels . . . a confusion of delight amidst which the breasts of the Greek horses are seen blazing in their breadth of golden strength".

All this and much more awaited Angelica on her peregrinations through Venice. She was particularly attracted by the pictures of Paolo Veronese with their inexhaustible inventiveness in grouping and the breathtaking use of colour. But even Venice and its colour could not lure her away from her chosen objective and she was soon at work on two historical pictures commissioned by English visitors.

Light entertainment was also not lacking; it seemed that all the world passed through Venice. During five hundred years the Council of Ten had ruled the State and had seen the growth of its resplendent history, ruler of the Adriatic, one of the principal markets of the western world, Eastern outlet. But now this great city was approaching the end of its glory; to its established splendour was succeeding a frivolous and corrupt society, intent on pleasure, full of intrigue, dissolute and elegant, where strangers, there for the moment, could find either the treasures of art or the most vicious debauchery. Wives betrayed their husbands, lovers their mistresses. In fact the position of women in the Republic had never been lower. Most of the noble ladies had been brought up in convents but the last thing they acquired there was education in the true sense. Dancing, singing and reciting verses were far more important. Each of the fashionable convents was presided over by a great lady as Mother Superior; in one it was a Dandolo, in another a Rezzonico, both most noble families; but they tolerated the visits of the vicious men of the town, and the grilles behind which the assumed young virgins talked to them only added to the piquancy of the occasion. In the pictures of Guardi and Longhi, to say nothing of the revelations of Casanova, we can meet it all. It must have shocked Angelica. Fortunately she had her work to attend to and romance was still to be found; or, if not the actual thing, then imagined romance, listening on some still evening to the song of the gondoliers, or drifting down the canal under a tender moon, forgetful of certain aspects of the life around her which contrasted too sharply with her strict German upbringing.

To further herself, however, it was essential for her to participate in the numerous *Ridotti* and in the social occasions where she might meet her noble clients. It must

have been at one of these that she was presented to the wife
of the English Ambassador, Lady Wentworth. She was the
daughter of Sir Ralph Milbanke Bart. and her first husband
was Sir Butler Cavendish Wentworth, who had died in
1741. She then married Mr. John Murray, His Majesty's
Resident in Venice from 1754 to 1756, retaining as a
courtesy title her former name. Lady Wentworth very
much enjoyed playing the hostess in London society, and
she foresaw the kudos which would be hers if she could
introduce this paragon of talent, intelligence and beauty to
England as her protégée. She offered to take Angelica to
her home where she would be certain of many more commissions and at far better prices than she was getting in
Italy, for the Italians much preferred to sell their own
painters' work than to support that of foreign artists. Lady
Wentworth, however, did not include in her invitation
Joseph Johann. He could follow later, but the initial success
must be hers alone. Father and daughter long debated the
move. They had never been separated; he had watched over
his "angel" with unremitting love. Was she to be taken
from him now? But Angelica was no longer an undeveloped
young girl. She was twenty-four, in full enjoyment of her
powers both as a woman and an artist, and she might well
have been daunted at the thought of an old man who spoke
no English going with her and watching her every move.
Whatever the deciding factors were, Lady Wentworth
prevailed, and she and Angelica set off for England. They
arrived in 1765 or 1766, more probably the latter, for they
stopped in Paris where Angelica was deeply impressed by
the paintings of Rubens, there to be seen in all the glory of
his colouring and luxuriant form. The first picture that
Angelica ever showed in London was the "Portrait of a
Gentleman" in the Exhibition of Free Artists in 1765. It was
catalogued as from "Miss Angelica Kaffmann in Rome"
and a note in one catalogue states that it was of David
Garrick. It may be asked how she could have painted the
great actor before she had been in England, but in 1763 he
had visited Italy and stayed in Rome and Naples.
Angelica's portrait of Garrick is in full accord with that of

Pompeo Batoni which must have been done about the same time. And as proof that she met him in Italy we have a note from Heinric Fuseli in a letter to his father in Zurich 1764: "I do not remember ever having seen a more beautiful portrait than that of the actor David Garrick (who is now in Naples) from the hand of Angelica." In Fitzgerald's life of Garrick there is a verse said to have been written by Garrick while he was sitting for the portrait:

> "While thus you paint with ease and grace
> And spirit all your own
> Take if you please my mind and face
> BUT LET MY HEART ALONE."

A further indication that the date of her arrival was in 1766 is in a letter to her father dated 11 July. She kept him well-informed of her movements. It is customary to write of Joseph Johann Kauffmann in a patronising if not actually hostile spirit, depicting him first as an over fond parent and then as a senile drag on his daughter's freedom of movement. But Angelica's portrait of him in the Landesmuseum in Innsbruck shows a face of strength and dignity, and, if he was anything like his portrait, he was far from being a nonentity. To Joseph Johann she wrote now: "I have been told many times that the English, when you meet them in their own country, are apt to forget all the promises of Friendship which they made when abroad, but I find this to be quite untrue and my experience is altogether opposed to this false statement. The gentlemen particularly are most kind (*molto gentili*), and their kindness is quite *sincere*, and, generally speaking, their words are full of good sense."

She was fortunate in her introduction to the town. Lady Wentworth's house in Hill Street was in a quarter which was becoming fashionable through the exploitation by speculative builders of the open fields which had previously been used for the May Fair. Near her was the house which Henry Holland had designed for General Burgoyne whose American campaign was to be

Two oval plaques in the Gallery of Harewood House, Leeds. Courtesy of the Earl of Harewood.

so damaging for England.[1] We may be sure that Lady Wentworth lost no time in introducing her protégée to society. Angelica was lucky too in the friendships she had formed in Rome: Lord Exeter, who gave her immediately an introduction to Reynolds, and Lady Spenser whose portrait she painted, helped to bring in commissions. But more than all it was her own personality which aided her. She had the sweetness of expression which fashion then valued so highly in a woman, a naturalness of manner and, for all her success, a modesty which appealed as much to women as to men. And doubtless her reputation for inspiring love was known too and did not lessen the interest in her. Beyond all this there was a tenacious character, a capacity for hard work and determination to succeed which was to be a lifelong characteristic.

We get a good idea of her effect on society in a letter written two years later by Count Bernsdorff,[2] to a friend: "She (Angelica) has a peculiar and most womanly dignity which inspires the utmost respect. She is about 27, by no means a Beauty, but extremely attractive. The character of her face belongs to the type Domenichino loved to paint; the features are noble, the expression sweet; it would be impossible to pass such a face without looking at it, and having looked, you must admire, and there are moments when she is absolutely beautiful; thus, when she is seated at her harmonia, singing Pergolesi's *Stabat Mater*, her large expressive eyes are piously raised to Heaven, her inspired look helps the expression of the divine words. At this moment she is a living St. Cecilia." This and similar testimony from other sources makes it clear that Angelica was well set to take the town by storm.

---

[1] This house, now 10 Hertford Street, has recently been renovated by the Equity and Law Life Assurance Company and shows some of Angelica's first decorations. It is almost certain that Reynolds recommended her to Robert Adam who was Holland's choice for decorator.

[2] The Danish Prime Minister and a great friend of the Prince of Wales, "Poor Fred".

5

The England to which Angelica came in 1766 was a country at peace, rich and prosperous. In 1760, George II had died, to be succeeded by his grandson. He had always preferred his Hanoverian possession to that of his English throne. The young George was the first really English King; brought up in England he declared that he wanted nothing to do with Hanover, "That horrid Electorate which had so long preyed on the vitals of this poor country", and he had also declared that he would bring to an end the "bloody and expensive war with France"—the Seven Years' War. But the war had brought England vast possessions, both in the West and in the East: Guadeloupe, the richest of the French sugar islands, and still more important Canada, where in 1758 an English fleet had captured Louisberg at the mouth of the St. Lawrence river, to be followed by the taking of Fort Duquesne. After months of fighting Wolfe laid siege to Quebec where finally in September he made his last attempt to take the town, whose Heights had so far defeated him. During the night of 15th and 16th, five thousand men with muffled oars had rowed past the French batteries to the cliffs behind the town and at break of day they scrambled up and overpowered the sentries. The French, surprised, fought back bravely but after a day's battle they were overpowered and the town was taken. Wolfe lay dead but his victory was complete, and when the news reached London the town went mad, the bells were rung till, as Horace Walpole said, they must be threadbare. Benjamin West celebrated his victory and death in his great picture, "The Death of Wolfe".

All this was to contribute presently to England's prosperity and stability. In the East, Clive had taken Madras and a number of French ports in India. And in 1758 Admiral Hawke had defeated a French fleet which was attempting to invade England. Now the young King began his reign by setting his old tutor, the Earl of Bute, at the head of his Government, and in doing so offended both Pitt and Newcastle who had led the fight against France. William Pitt, the Great Commoner as he has been called, considered himself the voice of the people, had been all for the war, as had Newcastle, a devoted minister of the late King. They both opposed Bute's proposal to make peace with France; the King was set on peace and both resigned. In 1763, however, a treaty was signed in Paris and the war came to an end. Guadeloupe was restored to the French and they kept their trading posts in India, but the East India Company retained their empire in the sub-continent. And above all, England kept Canada, except for a small enclave in the East. Montreal and Quebec remained French. The King, although he had succeeded in his design for peace, had to face the prospect of a determined party in Parliament whom he had offended, and he became as hated by the Whigs as his grandfather had been approved of.

While all this was happening, the social side of English life had received an impetus with the coming of George III. Gone were the heavy Georgian Kings with their obnoxious mistresses and their contempt for the arts. "I hate bainting and boetry," announced George II, and painting and poetry suffered in consequence. Now better things seemed in view, and in 1762 Horace Walpole could write, "If there are any talents among us this seems the crisis for their appearance. The Throne itself is the altar of the Graces, and whoever sacrifices to them becomingly is sure that his offering will be smiled upon by a prince who is at once the example and patron of Accomplishments." This may seem only a fulsome tribute, but it was a fact that the Arts had taken on a new life, and the galaxy of talent, not to say genius, which flowered in the last years of the century has seldom been surpassed. It was Angelica's good fortune to arrive just then; as Flaxman was to say of her, "she was of the time and the time was made for her".

London provided something of a different aspect from the Italian towns Angelica was accustomed to. To begin with, there was the climate. Then as now it was variable and mostly inclement. "I have been confined these three weeks with a fever," wrote Lord Hervey in April 1743, "which is the annual tribute my detestable constitution pays to our detestable climate at the return of every Spring". The rainy and gloomy days did not add to the amenities of London, for though the water flushed the roadways the damp rotted the heaps of decaying rubbish. And yet the mixture of urban splendour and rural charm may have satisfied the country-bred Angelica, for not so far away from Lady Wentworth's fashionable house stretched the meadows and farms of Marylebone, where the pleasure gardens drew the elegant crowds of a fine evening and the view away towards Highgate and Hampstead could be enjoyed.

The disagreeable features of life in towns are always accepted by those who dwell in them, and no doubt for Angelica, who was immediately introduced by her patroness to the most elevated circles, the minor discomforts of life faded into the background. Lady Wentworth insisted on taking her to her dressmaker and hairdresser and in no time we see a transformation. She shared, says a writer of the time, "with hoops of extra magnitude, toupees of superabundant floweriness, shoe heels of vividest scarlet and china monsters of superlative ugliness, the privilege of being the rage". Without going to the lengths indicated in this quotation, Angelica appears in her portrait by Reynolds as a fashionable lady. And by August 1766 we have Lady Mary Coke writing to her sister, Lady Stafford, "I went to Lady Ailesbury's and found her and Mr. Conway were going to a paintress who is just arrived from Italy, and was brought over by Lady Wentworth, the same who drew a picture of Mr. Garrick, which was shown I am told in the Exhibition (of the Society of Free Artists). I went with them and saw the picture she was painting of Miss Conway (now eighteen). It was like, and appeared to be well done, but too large, as you would take it for a very big woman."

As well as the Society to which Lady Wentworth

introduced her, the patrons who had known Angelica in
Rome took her up at once. Lord Exeter brought her
quickly to the notice of Reynolds. He was an immediate
conquest. Not only did he find her charming but he approved her talent and the suggestion that they should paint
each other's portraits almost certainly came from him.
Commendation could go no further, and the Press, ever
ready to notice a new fashion, wrote in the *Public
Advertiser*:

> While fair Angelica with matchless grace
> Paints Conway's lovely form and Stanhope's face
> Our hearts to beauty willing homage pay
> We praise, admire, and gaze our souls away.

The most immediate thing for the artist now was to find
a suitable dwelling and not impose longer than necessary on
her protectress's hospitality, especially as the latter had not
been well. Among the first people she had met in London
were her father's friend, George Moser, and his daughter
Mary. Moser had come when still young to England and
established himself as a chaser and painter on enamel. His
daughter was a painter of flowers, highly thought of and
much appreciated by Queen Charlotte. This good family
welcomed Angelica warmly and the two girls became close
friends. They probably helped her in her search for rooms,
which she eventually found in Suffolk Street, Charing
Cross, in a house belonging to a surgeon. From here she
wrote to her father, who obviously was anxiously waiting to
know where and when he might join her.

"I am here with good people, old acquaintances of Lady
Wentworth, who had the goodness to recommend me to
them as if I were her own daughter. I have been a month
here. The people of the house do everything for me, the
lady is a mother to me, and her two daughters love me as
a sister . . . it was such a good opportunity and suited me
so well that I did not hesitate to take the rooms for a
whole winter. I have four rooms, one where I paint and a
second where I hang my finished pictures—for it is the

custom here for people to come and view the paintings
without disturbing the artist. The other two rooms are
very small. One of them is my bedroom, though there is
hardly room in it for the bedstead, and in the other I
keep my clothes and other such things. For the rooms I
pay two guineas a week, and one guinea for the food and
the servant, whose clothes I also provide. This is without
washing and other small daily expenses. I could not do
without a servant. These are my expenses which will not
seem small to you, but they could not be lower. I am sure
if you come this winter we will have to take a house,
which is very hard to find. Under a hundred guineas
there is nothing to be had—unfurnished I mean, of
course. And to furnish a house as they do here would
cost us another four hundred guineas. Think how expensive all this would be, especially in winter when everything is much dearer, and the days are short, so that one
cannot get much done."

Think, also, she might have added, how many pictures
will have to be painted to provide such sums of money.
Even Reynolds, then at the height of his popularity, only
asked a fee of forty guineas, and Angelica was barely at the
beginning of her fame. She went on to insist further in an
effort to defer her father's joining her immediately, saying
that if he were there they would need a man *and* a maid
servant. She may also have feared the effects of the climate
on her father's poor health. How could she work and at the
same time look after a sick old man? And though she did
not say it, what would she do with someone who did not
speak a word of English, and who did not know the town or
its ways? Her letter, for all its expressions of devotion, is a
little disingenuous. One has a feeling that she is not averse
to being out of leading strings at last, to be free to enjoy her
growing success, and the new friends she is making. Nevertheless, all the arguments advanced in it were absolutely
true.

London had much to offer in this summer of 1766, as
she pointed out to Joseph Johann. She was getting known

to "everyone here". That meant not only to the serious patrons but to the dilettante young men about town who loved to lounge away an hour or two in some studio, especially if the painter was young and pretty. Then too the daughters of the aristocracy, always on the look out for husbands, found an artist's studio neutral ground where they could hear and retail the latest gossip and the best rehearsed *jeu d'esprit*, what Mr. Walpole had said, and what the ravishing Perdita (Mrs. Robinson) had worn on her last outing in the Park.

Soon the nobles would disperse to their country seats, where they would proceed with the building of their enormous new houses and recover from the season's profligate misuse of time and money. The houses at least were greatly to the advantage of architects, painters and furniture makers. The fashions, copying the mode in France, were outrageous. According to Walpole, Edward Wortley Montague, a typical beau, "Walked with his buttons and buckles bediamonded, belaced and be-wigged, worth £2,500, and more besnuffed-boxed than would suffice a Chinese idol with a hundred noses", while the ladies smeared themselves with cosmetics to achieve the desired delicacy of a white skin. We little think when we admire the beauties of the time in their portraits by Reynolds or Gainsborough that their faces were so thick with mercury water and white lead that some even died of the poison. The two beautiful Gunning sisters perished from this habit, but nothing would break women of it. Soon Angelica succumbed to the temptation of fine clothes and hairdressing, but she wore no powder and all her self portraits show her natural colouring.

Her need for patrons forced her to live largely in this world; but her youth and good spirits helped her to enjoy its pleasures. Nevertheless her natural taste led her far more in the direction of that other society open to her through her friendship with Reynolds, the man of whom Samuel Johnson had said, "If I should lose him, I should lose the only man I can truly call a friend."

Born in 1721 he was such a prodigy that he was
early sent to London to study with Hudson, the portrait
painter, but left him because of his instructor's jealousy.
He returned to his native Devonshire in 1743 and
began portrait painting. While in Plymouth he had the
good fortune to paint the fashionable Miss Chudleigh
and her admirer Captain Lepell who, when he was
appointed to the Mediterranean station, took Reynolds
with him. He went to Algiers and Morocco, painting all
the officers, and finally arrived in Rome, where he
studied the works of the great masters. This he did for
his own development, resolutely refusing to make copies
for sale. He returned to England in 1752 and took a
house in St. Martin's Lane. His brother artists saw him
for what he was, a very great man; but public recognition came slowly. The charming painter Liotard had
recently arrived from Paris, and was all the rage. But a
master such as Reynolds had only to wait; success,
when it came, was overwhelming. He was to end by
being the arbiter of the artistic world in England and,
incidentally, was to make a great deal of money. In 1764
he moved to a house in Leicester Square and set up
there in splendour; his dinners were famous, and no
wonder, with such men as Johnson, Goldsmith, Garrick,
Burke and Gibbon, to name but a few. Talk must have
been superlative, and wit a constant incentive to imagination.

There was of course some criticism of his painting.
No successful artist is immune from it. It had been
stated that Dr. Johnson aided Sir Joshua in the composition of his Discourses, a charge firmly denied by
others. It had also been said that Reynolds was careless
about his pigments and used too much carmine, think-
ing he could "shut it in with varnish". The same was
said of Angelica, and we shall see how the colour in the
picture she painted of the Duchess of Weimar faded and
how Goethe wrote asking how and with what they could
replace the varnish. One must admit, however, that
today there is no sign of deterioration in Angelica's best

paintings, or justification in her case for the gibe by one
of the journals of the time at Reynolds' expense:

> The art of painting was at first designed
> To bring the dead, our ancestors to mind.
> But this same painter has reversed the plan
> And made the portrait die before the man.

All Lady Wentworth's hopes for her protégée were
being fulfilled. To get the reception from society which she
was getting set the seal on Angelica's success. She was soon
known to all the best painters of the day, and commissions
for portraits flowed in. She indulged in beautiful clothes
and elegant hair arrangements, as we see in her self-
portraits of the time, but excused her extravagance with the
plea that if she went to fashionable houses she must be
suitably dressed. Poor Nathaniel Dance seems to have been
quickly jettisoned. Her treatment of him raises the question
once more: was she, or was she not a coquette? To give an
answer one must consider the various factors involved and
then make a reasonable guess. If there was ever any
documentary evidence, Angelica burnt it in Rome with
other papers towards the end of her life. She would certainly seem to have behaved badly to Dance. But the basic
goodness of her nature as revealed by Goethe, Herder and
others, makes that assumption out of character. On the
other hand, they knew her after much suffering could have
changed her radically. It is notable that her early German
biographers are singularly hostile to Angelica. They do not
state a specific grievance but again and again in a sneer or
an implication they make this hostility plain. Steinberg sees
her departure to England as in itself an abandonment of
substance for shadow. He accuses her of sacrificing her art
for love of pleasure and greed of gain. Opperman hints at
that early love, unspecified, which might have made her
happy had she not abandoned happiness in favour of ambition. The real grievance of these writers may have been
that she appeared to prefer Italians and English to those
good Germanic roots where her talent had had its origin.
Steinberg said of the Englishman that whatever artistic

treasures he possessed he covered with the ashes of a cold egoism. In contrast to the Frenchman and the Italian, "He locks up his picture in his own gallery under the care of a surly guardian. He never sees it himself; he is content to have been the purchaser, the one who has money enough to outbid others, and who has bought *a very dear picture*. With this all is said and done!"

Even if we allow for a tincture of malice in her German commentators, we are under the obligation to face one simple fact, that Angelica was, of necessity, a careerist. It is this that may explain her rather incomprehensible behaviour where love was concerned. It is possible that she was not passionate by nature and that even as a young woman she felt herself wedded primarily to her art. But, with her intelligence, she would know that she could not afford to reveal this particular trait to her admirers or to her social patrons. It would have labelled her as a freak and they might have lost interest in her immediately. She must play the part, and it was not a very difficult part for a young and attractive woman of her age to play. Besides, she would scarcely have been human if she had not welcomed at least some admiration for its own sake.

All this would be sufficient to explain her acceptance of Dance's attentions in Rome. He was not only a wealthy connoisseur, able to travel and to indulge his taste for beautiful things but he was also a distinctly talented artist whose work is still respected today. His self-portrait in the National Portrait Gallery reveals a rather austere individual with a grave penetrating eye, but he could well be called handsome. And in the Landesmuseum in Bregenz is an unfinished portrait by Angelica of a nameless but handsome young man, who may well be Dance for his features definitely correspond with those of Dance's self-portrait in London. In a letter to her father, she mentions that she has had a flattering proposal but seems almost to pride herself upon its rejection. She does not mention any name, but if it had been Dance, whom he knew, she would surely have said so.

Perhaps she loved him. Perhaps in Rome she thought

that she might well come to love him. But in England and fallen under the spell of the appreciative Reynolds, she might feel differently. It has been suggested repeatedly that she hoped for a proposal from Reynolds and so sent Dance about his business. Reynolds was her senior by eighteen years but that is not an insuperable impediment. He had known and painted very many beautiful women, he enjoyed their company but he was very far from being either a susceptible youngster or an elderly philanderer. He may have enjoyed Angelica's youthful charm but what he really appreciated was her exceptionable talent. In fact—after the London gossips had had their say on these two painting each other's portraits and perhaps after noticing signs of undue warmth on Angelica's part—it is fairly plain that he drew back for a time, until the situation had clarified itself, and so preserved a lasting friendship. It is monstrous to suggest, as Wurzbach has done, that he afterwards joined in a conspiracy to humiliate her.

As for Angelica, he had been a hero to her from the start and in an early letter to Joseph Johann, on the London artists, she wrote, "but Mr. Reynolds is the finest of them all, a very great master. His manner of painting is quite his own, and his portraits are mostly historical. He has a flying pencil (*pennello volante*) which gives a fine effect of light and shade."

Soon she was at work on her portrait of him and the *Public Advertiser* quickly took note of the fact thus:

> "But when the likeness she has done of thee,
> O Reynolds with astonishment we see;
> Forced to submit, with all our pride we own
> Such strength, such harmony, excelled by none,
> And thou art rivalled by thyself alone."

The praise may have been too generous. Some of her fellow artists may have felt more disposed to echo Goldsmith's witty verse, with its side-blow at publicists, when, being invited at the last minute to a party to which both Reynolds and Angelica were going, he wrote in reply:

"Your mandate I got
You may all go to pot
For sending so late
To one of my state,
But 'tis Reynolds's way
From wisdom to stray
And Angelica's whim
To be frolic like him.
But alas, your good worships
How could they be wiser,
When both have been spoiled
In today's Advertiser."

It is hard, as we have said, not to see Dance's drawing of these two in the studio, Sir Joshua with hand raised to a deaf ear, and Angelica a rather sharp-featured spinster, as the semi-satirical revenge of a rejected and embittered suitor. And Angelica herself can be forgiven if for a time she misinterpreted the situation. Everyone was making a fuss of her, and, considering all the great painter's attentions to her, she can hardly be blamed. In his note book he referred to her as Miss Angel, and there is an entry "Fiori" (flowers) whether to remind himself to send them or for some other more intimate purpose. He loved a pretty woman, and he really may have been captivated by Angelica's undoubted charm and spirit. He certainly could not have felt in any danger from her success. But Reynolds had been known to say that an artist married is an artist ruined, and indeed every artist knows that a wife at his side very rarely helps him with feminine admirers. And these were Reynolds's chief stock in trade. Also it must never be forgotten that Reynolds, for all his worldliness, was a very great and dedicated artist; his Discourses to his students bear this out. They may seem a little out-of-date to readers now, but they still contain so much wisdom and breathe such a penetrating atmosphere of devotion to his art that one can understand the elevated position which he held. At the end of his fifteenth Discourse these were his parting words, after speaking of his veneration for Michelangelo. "I feel a self-congratulation in knowing myself capable of such sensations as he intended to excite. I reflect, not without vanity, that these Discourses bear testimony of my admiration of that truly divine man; and I should desire that the last words I should pronounce in this Academy and from this place, might be the name of—Michelangelo."

Angelica worked hard during this winter. It was necessary to make money in order that her promise to her father could be kept, and in fact in 1767 she was able to buy a house in Golden Square, then quite a fashionable neighbourhood. If its tenants did not reach the eminence of the nearby Soho Square, still Mrs. Delany had lived close by in Hog Lane, and other distinguished women were her neighbours. The houses in this charming Square are all gone now excepting two, and it would be pleasant to imagine that Angelica had lived in one of them, possibly Number 11. But J. T. Smith asserts that she chose a house on the south side of the Square, so as to profit by the north light, so necessary for painters, and, as she said to her father, the days were short in this dull city. Shortly after she moved there she received a most flattering commission from the King's sister, the Duchess of Brunswick, to paint her portrait. It was a success, and from that moment she was made. The house in Golden Square was besieged with imperious clients, and when it was known that the Princess of Wales had visited her to see the portrait, the crowds became even larger. Golden Square was blocked. Angelica was in a delirium of extravagant delight and wrote her father, "Never oh never has any painter received such a distinguished visitor." Letter followed letter. "There is nothing but praise for my work: even the papers are full of verses written in different languages, all in praise of me and my pictures." And again, "I have finished some portraits which meet great approval. Mr. Reynolds is more pleased than anyone. I have painted his portrait, which has succeeded wonderfully, and will do me credit; it will be engraved immediately. Lady Spenser has paid one hundred ducats for her picture. Lord Exeter is still in the country. This morning I had a visit from Mr. Garrick. My Lady Spenser

was with me two days ago. My Lord Baltimore visits me
sometimes. The Queen has only returned two days, as soon
as she is better I am to be presented to her. Two days ago
the Duchess of Ancaster came to see me. She is the first
lady at Court."

When Lord Exeter returned to town he became one of
her most devoted patrons, and in the wonderful collections
at Burghley House may be seen today some of her finest
pictures. There too is a delightful portrait of Angelica as
she was in these first days in London, painted by Nathaniel
Dance, presumably before he had received his congé. It
shows her without her version of the exaggerated hair styles
of the day, in a pretty grey silk gown, pencil in hand, half
grave, half smiling, an intimate portrait of a much admired
young woman. She looks the part. No wonder she was
excited, no wonder she felt the equal of anyone, and no
wonder also that, being the talk of the Town, her fellow
artists' tongues were not always so laudatory. Her "Portrait
of Reynolds" was in fact not as good as she professed it to
be. She did not finish it till 1769 and it is not certain
whether and where it was ever exhibited.

6

Reynolds drew back gracefully for a time. As for Dance, he married a Mrs. Douver, a rich widow and in 1801 he was made a baronet and changed his name to Holland. We may consider ourselves lucky that for one reason or another Angelica refused to marry him; her life and her career would have suffered and we are relieved to think that at this point, with such professional success at her feet, she chose once more Art rather than marriage, though union with Reynolds might have combined both. There was another pretender to her hand who would have been even less successful as a husband. This was Henry Fuseli, who was madly in love with her, but in this case his passionate unbalanced nature, together with his poverty, must have been disagreeable to her.

There are a number of contradictory accounts both of his character and his appearance. We are told that he was "always in love with a different woman . . . a dandy and possessed of a ready wit . . . a small man, broad-shouldered and well-proportioned, with large blue eyes, of an intellectual and energetic aspect and always exceptionally polite to women, with at the same time a considerable idea of his own importance". Another account makes him "singularly handsome with a wonderful genius which would naturally attract a girl of Angelica's romantic temperament", although actually this does not seem to have been the case. According to his biographer Knowles, his conception of the deity was a particularly sublime one and he "seldom took up the Bible, which he frequently did, without shedding tears". According to his friend, the poet William Blake, Fuseli was "damned good to steal from" (artistically) and he has the benefit of one of Blake's cryptic epigrams, which were seldom complimentary, but which in this case can be regarded as almost gracious.

> The only man that e'er I knew
> Who did not make me almost spew
> Was Fuseli! he was both Turk and Jew
> And so, dear Christian friends, how do ye do?

Perhaps Blake meant that to his conventional English acquaintances Fuseli was suspect as both a foreigner and as an unconventional artist. There was, of course, no connection with either Constantinople or Jerusalem. Fuseli had been born in Zurich in 1741 (the same year as Angelica) and christened Johann Heinrich Füsli; but we shall refer to him here as Henry Fuseli, the name which he adopted when he took up residence in England. He had a cousin in Zurich, another Johann Heinrich Füsli, who accompanied Winckelmann on his more or less clandestine trip to Naples—disapproved by jealous local archaeologists—in 1764 and Henry Fuseli's father, Hans Caspar Füsli was a portraitist and miniaturist and had collected funds for Winckelmann's earlier trip to the same city in 1758. Fuseli himself was to translate Winckelmann's *Reflections on the Painting and Sculpture of the Greeks* in 1765. He was an accomplished individual and held an M.A. from a Swiss university. Like Angelica, he had been a juvenile prodigy and, like her, he had come to England under the protection of an English patron. He arrived in 1763 with Sir Andrew Mitchell, British Minister to the Prussian Court. Again it was Reynolds who launched him on the road to recognition, and extolled his work to all his friends. But Reynolds was not alone in this high opinion of the Switzer. Lawrence collected Fuseli's paintings, gave him kinship with Michelangelo and said that there had been nothing like him since the fifteenth and sixteenth centuries. And Benjamin Haydon would later write: "Fuzeli (sic) was undoubtedly the greatest genius of that day . . . he was a monster in design, his women are all strumpets, and his men all banditti, with

Self portrait. Courtesy of the Uffizi Gallery, rence.

2. Self portrait. Courtesy of the National Portrait Gallery, London.

Nathaniel Dance: Joshua Reynolds with Angelica etail). Courtesy of the Earl of Harewood, rewood House, Leeds.

4. Johann Peter Kauffmann. Bust of Angelica. Courtesy of the Protomoteca Capitolina, Rome.

5, 6. (left) A classical Greek statue which Angelica studied and drew with Winkelmann, in reaction against the high Baroque as typified by the Bernini statue above. Both are in the Borghese Gallery, Rome. For further influences, see illustrations 49-51.

A. Das Hof zu Chur. B. Das Schloß. C. Die Bischoffliche Domkirch. D. S. Lucia. E. S. Martins Pfarrkirch. F. Prediger Clorter. G. Das Rahthauß. H. Das Kauffhauß. I. S. Regula Pfarrkirch. K. Plesser fluß. L. Der Rhein fluß. M. Schloß Haldenstein.

7. Chur: Angelica's birthplace. In 1741 the town would not have looked very different from this print of 1642. Courtesy of the Rätisches Museum, Chur.

8. Golden Square viewed from the south. Courtesy of Messrs. Rye, Lawrence & Leman, Golden Square

9. The Piazza di Spagna and the Spanish Steps.

10. The Villa Albani.

11. A landscape by Zucchi at Nostell Priory. Courtesy of Lord St. Oswald.

12. The Marino at Clontarf built by Lord Charlemont. It is typical of the neo-classical style. Photo: Clair Studios, Dublin.

13. Nostell Priory near Wakefield in 1829.

14. Johann Georg Schütz: Duchess Anna Amelia with friends (including Angelica Kauffmann, in the garden of the Villa d'Este. Courtesy of Die Nationale Forschungs-und Gedenkstätten der klassischen deutschen Literatur, Weimar.

15. J. J. Kauffmann. A portrait of her father by Angelica. Courtesy of the Tiroler Landesmuseum Ferdinandeum, Innsbruck.

16. Angelica's portrait of Antonio Zucchi, her second husband. Courtesy of R. Winkler, Kilchberg.

17. David Garrick. Courtesy of the Marquess of Exeter, Burghley House, Stamford.

18. Prince Poniatowski in 1786. Courtesy of Andrea Busiri Vici.

19. The Bariatinsky family. Courtesy of the Vorarlberger Landesmuseum, Bregenz.

20. Johann Wolfgang von Goethe. Courtesy of Die Nationale Forschungs-und Gedenkstätten der klassischen deutschen Literatur, Weimar.

21. The nymph presiding in the Temple of Immortality receives from two swans the few names, engraved on gold and silver medals, that they have saved from those thrown into the river Lethe by Time. Courtesy of Federico Zeri.

22. Hibernia. The figure was used as the basis of the seal of the Bank of Ireland. It is said that the sitter was the daughter of an engineer in the Bank Printing Office. Courtesy of the Bank of Ireland.

23. Maddalena Riggi. Courtesy of the Freies Deutsches Hochstift, Frankfurter Goethemuseum.

the action of galvanised frogs, the dress of mountebanks and the hue of pestilential putridity."

Though Fuseli resembled Angelica in his mastery of languages, his wide reading and his choice of historical subjects, their art could not have been more diverse. He was a fantastic creature with a prolific imagination and a strong fierce brush, producing monstrous nightmare subjects but with a conviction and genius only equal to that of Blake himself. In 1769 he went to Italy with a companion with whom he quarrelled on the ship, and he continued on to Rome alone. Here he threw himself into study, particularly of the work of Michelangelo whose grandeur and freedom influenced his style. He made extraordinary progress in drawing and to this end he attended Schools of Anatomy and even used the dissecting knife in order to trace the muscles of the body. He left no stone unturned in order to progress and when he returned to London in 1779 he found his place among the most admired artists. But he was not an easy man to be friendly with. One said of him, "I will now introduce you to a most ingenious foreigner whom I think you will like, but if you wish to enjoy his conversation you will not attempt to stop the torrent of his words by contradicting him". His wit and gibes at fellow artists, his wild and unpremeditated flights of fancy, and his intemperate passions were tolerated because of his learning and love of poetry and art. He determined to show that he could paint as well or better than West, with more invention and boldness of drawing, and he pursued anything which might stimulate these qualities. It is to this period that possibly belong the extraordinary pornographic drawings which have prompted the question: was he a pervert? To which the answer is that his addiction to the Bible—to say nothing of his marriage to a wife with whom he was happy for thirty-five years—would seem to give the lie. It is more likely that he found in the extraordinary attitudes of his subjects the material for his often contorted figures.

Fuseli's first great success had been his painting *The Nightmare*. The original sketch lacked the horse's head, and had only the elongated and agonised figure of the

4—AK * *

young girl. It was followed by "The Weird Sisters" and "Macbeth". These were all subjects involving horror. His criticism of West's picture, "Hubert and Arthur", shows clearly the trend of his own mind. Northcote depicts Hubert overwhelmed by a wave of remorseful pity. Fuseli commented, "West has taken the wrong moment, for whoever looks at the hesitating Hubert must see that the boy is safe, the danger past and the interest gone. West should have chosen the moment when Hubert stamps his foot and cries, 'Come forth, do as I bid you', and the two ruffians should have appeared brandishing red hot irons. Then the scene would have been as it ought to have been—terrible."

It was to this extraordinary man that Angelica was introduced probably by George Moser, the old friend of Joseph Johann who had a daughter Mary, a clever painter of flowers and similar subjects. Mary was deeply in love with Fuseli. But she was a plain girl, her affection was not returned by him and the extraordinary thing is that she is said to have quarrelled later with Angelica not on any grounds of stealing the affections of someone to whom she was so devoted but apparently for her unkindness in refusing him! Feminine devotion to an idol could hardly go further. At any rate refuse him Angelica did, and Fuseli is accused of revealing his chagrin in a verdict which he subsequently passed upon her painting, when he remarked, "I have no wish to contradict those who make success the standard of genius—and as their heroine equals the greatest names in the past (i.e. in the acclaim which she received) suppose her on a level with them in power. The Germans, with as much patriotism at least as judgement, have styled her the paintress of the soul; nor can this be wondered at; for a nation who, in an Anton Raphael Mengs, flatter themselves that they possess an artist equal to Raphael the divine." This is cutting enough in all conscience, to come from a rejected lover; and for good weight there is thrown in the sideblow at Mengs.

7

Marriage with Fuseli would have been like union with a volcano. But these love affairs were very unimportant in the artist's life compared with the work to which she was devoted and which certainly employed most of her time. Her father was of course as intoxicated as she was by all this success. It is said that he carried her letters with him everywhere and read them to all who would listen; everyone in Schwarzenberg knew about them. He knew too about her many suitors and must have rejoiced that she was so wedded to her art, for he had sunk all his hopes in her future as a great artist. So when she assured him, "Not so easily will I bind myself. Rome is ever in my thoughts. May the Spirit of God guide me," he felt reassured and prepared to join his successful child in London.

"Rome is ever in my thoughts." Even Rossi, who quotes the letter, is not quite certain what she meant by these words. He interprets them as signifying that she was wholly devoted to her art. But if so, why bring Rome into it unless she meant that it was in Rome that her eyes had been first opened to the beauty of painting—which would not be true—or to the beauty of the antique—which would be largely irrelevant. Incidentally, Winckelmann's canon could be pedantic and full of generalisations like: "After all, what does a woman have that is supposed to be so beautiful? . . . A magnificent bosom does not last, and besides Nature has made this part of the body not for beauty's sake, but for the nourishment of the young." Angelica's six words remain as cryptic as any utterance of the oracle at Delphi and if Rossi could not explain them, there is little or no chance of our being able to do so now.

Joseph Johann arrived in London in the early part of 1767 and brought with him his sister's daughter Rosa

Fiorini, to help and care for Angelica. The old man still painted a little, and was not above copying some of his daughter's works and passing them off as his own. But in general he occupied himself with arranging the studio for the thronging visitors and fussing over the household. He could share in her ever-growing success, and exult when she was presented at Court. Her prices too had increased, she could now ask twenty guineas for a portrait head and more for a full figure. It was now too that she began to paint the historical pictures for which she became so well known. It had always been her desire, but the necessity to make a living had prevented her from spending the thought and time needed for such work. Her first opportunity to exhibit such paintings came in 1768 when on the occasion of a visit from King Christian VII of Denmark the Society of Artists arranged in his honour a special exhibition. To this she sent three pictures: "Venus appearing to Aneas", "Penelope with the bow of Ulysses" and "Hector's taking leave of Andromache". This exhibition was only open for two days for invited guests, but in the following year, 1769, in the opening exhibition of the newly instituted Royal Academy of Arts she sent in the pictures again with a fourth, "Achilles discovered by Ulysses". They were hung together and are now to be seen in Saltram House.

These pictures brought her and Benjamin West the honour of being the initiators of the classical style of painting. West, other than Kauffmann, the first protagonist of this style, showed in the exhibition his two historic pictures, "Farewell of Regulus" and "Venus mourning the death of Adonis". Although the above-mentioned were her first pictures in this style, they are among her finest. Particularly Hector's farewell, in its noble portrayal of intense but restrained grief and its rich colouring reveals her as the apt pupil of Winckelmann and a student of the Venetian painters.

As Peter Walsh points out, it was one thing to paint the pictures, another thing to sell them. Even West had difficulty in persuading his patrons to invest in them. But here again Reynolds came to her aid. He found for her a

friend, John Parker of Saltram, later Lord Morley, whom
he had known since his youth in Plympton. This gentleman was persuaded to buy the whole series together with
thirteen Reynolds portraits. It is questionable whether
without this support Angelica could have continued to paint
the historical subjects, although we know that ever since her
stay in Rome this had been her aim and wish. None of the
other English painters who essayed this style was so
favoured as she. Gavin Hamilton sent a work from time to
time from Rome where he was actively engaged in archaeological work, and Nathaniel Dance also tried his hand at it,
but it fell to Angelica to be the chief exponent of the
neo-classical period in England.

We can imagine her at this time, elegant as in her
portrait by Reynolds, her hair dressed high, and threaded
with a few pearls, two long curls falling on her lovely neck
and shoulders. The large luminous eyes, the dignified pose
of the head, the firm line of the mouth and chin, all bespeak
a distinguished personality, and yet something so lovable,
so tender, that we readily understand her appeal to both
men and women. She would be a good listener, we feel, and
certainly she had the opportunity to hear some of the best
talk that any period has known. For round Reynolds's table
or in the charming home of Mr. and Mrs. Garrick at
Twickenham she could meet the stars of the stage, and all
her colleagues; not all at the same time however, for they
did not all love each other. Reynolds in particular could be
sarcastic on the subject. But in general they were united.
Opie thought that Reynolds was the greatest colourist he
had any knowledge of; Flaxman speaks of Romney as being
gifted with peculiar powers for historical and ideal painting;
in art Reynolds might excel him but not in simplicity: in a
word Romney strove to touch the heart, Reynolds to please
the eye. Dr. Johnson did not venture so far afield as
Twickenham, but his wit and wisdom enlivened many an
evening at Reynolds's house in Leicester Square. These
dinners were long and enormous. The courses still consisted
of from three to nine meat dishes and the same number of
side dishes. Ladies and gentlemen sat separately, for it was

necessary to guard the innocence of the young and the morals of the older ladies. Horace Walpole wrote, "I am still so antiquated as to dine at four when I can, though frequently prevented as so many are so good as to call on me at that hour because it is too soon for them to go home and dress so early in the morning (sic)." When the gentlemen rose from the table they joined the ladies in the withdrawing room, and then the real entertainment of the evening began, the wits of the day dispensed their well-rehearsed offering, the merits of writers and artists were discussed, and of course in fashionable circles gaming began.

As for the women Angelica met and painted, they fell into two categories: the intelligent and the butterflies. Lady Craven, afterwards the Margravine of Anspach, wrote, "to say the truth there is no part of the world where our sex is treated with so much contempt as England. I do not complain of men for having engrossed the Government; in excluding us from all degree of power they have saved us from fatigues, danger and perhaps many crimes . . . but I think it the highest injustice that the studies that raise the character of a man should be supposed to hurt that of a woman. We are educated in the grossest ignorance, and no art is omitted to stifle our natural reason . . . I am now speaking of our English notions which may wear out some day ages hence along with others equally absurd."

But there were other women who had by their exceptional gifts and perseverance raised themselves from such reproach. These were the Blue Stockings, chief among them the witty Mrs. Montague with her house in Hill Street, and Mrs. Delany, the friend of the Queen, who read Pliny and Epictetus, translated by the erudite Mrs. Carter, and who was also concerned with the poor situation of women. Then there were the gaming women, of whom the student of Epictetus wrote, "It mortifies my sex's pride to see them expose themselves so much to the contempt of men." But actually the men were equally spendthrift, both sexes losing vast sums in a night's play.

We can picture easily enough the social and artistic

circles in which she moved but it is a much harder if not an actually impossible task to form a conception of Angelica's personality at all its deeper levels. It is a curious thing that this woman who was admittedly a leading artist of the time, who was accepted in the most elevated literary and artistic circles, and even in the beginning in fashionable London, is hardly mentioned in the letters and journals of the time. We know that she was a frequent visitor at the home of Dr. Burney, and yet Miss Burney, in her voluminous diary mentions her only once. Mrs. Delany once, and Horace Walpole only curtly in notes in his catalogues. Farington, it is true, speaks of her at greater length, but never intimately. What could be the reason? Was she, in spite of her beauty and charm, not socially a success, was she more of a silent observer at parties, more of a listener than a talker? We know of course that no one is more popular in a society of eloquent talkers than a person who listens with pleasure and attention. Perhaps this is the clue: she looked beautiful, smiled and listened, and most people loved her. And at Dr. Burney's she could exercise her other gift, she could sing.

If this talented woman, centre of a blaze of popularity and fortunate in the attachment of a number of close personal friends, wanted to hide the secrets of her heart from posterity, she could hardly have been more successful than she has been. It is possible she did want this. If she burnt most of her personal papers when she left England, this would seem to be so. She was far from being indifferent to success. But, though they were very different in character, she may have valued her personal privacy as much as Jane Austen did hers. Neither of them was a Marie Bashkirtseff.

A number of possible explanations are available. The significant occasions in an individual's life are not so many, and if one has been able to close down on them and destroy any evidence in relation to them, it is like drawing a cloak of welcome invisibility about one's shoulders. This is just what Angelica would have most wished to do in relation to at least one episode in her life, and possibly to several others. Moreover, a great part of her life was spent as a bird of passage and this does not lend itself to an accumulation of documentary evidence. When Rossi came to write his memoir of her, which was first published in 1810 in Florence, he depended largely upon past hearsay obtained years before from the lips of her elderly father. The memory of an old man is not so reliable, and in particular of an old man whose resentment probably ran at an even deeper level than the victim's did, and who must have had an almost stronger inclination to bury that portion of his daughter's past, than the daughter herself.

But she wrote letters? And a number of them have survived? This is quite true, but she wrote letters at a time when an artificiality and exaggeration on paper was almost obligatory. Even friendly letters were a rhetorical exercise if not a formal display of wordy insincerity. In her correspondence at a much later date with Goethe, Angelica was not afraid to be herself and to reveal tendernesses and nostalgic regrets which are moving to us when we read them now. But she was a woman of forty-seven by then, writing to a famous man eight years younger than herself; and she had no need of dissimulation. She knew the warmth of his appreciation of her and he has left abundant testimony to it on paper. Every expression of friendship on her side, therefore, was perfectly seemly in the circumstances. He kept her letters but she destroyed his before she died, perhaps because they were too precious to her or perhaps because his had gradually become aloof and perfunctory after Christiane Vulpius made her appearance in his life.[1] Angelica's letters to Goethe are warm-hearted and the nearest we ever get to self-revelation in her correspondence but they come too late in the day and do not take us very far.

[1] By 1797 he was addressing her as "most honoured friend" and assuring her that if she will be good enough to lend Zucchi's biographical notes to "a most respectable tradesman in Leipzig" who was compiling an art catalogue "you will confer on me a new proof of your friendship". This last letter of his ends with the almost insulting formality of "Farewell and kindly answer either yourself or through others".

8

Among the men who idled away an hour or two in Angelica's London studio was one who stood out among the others. He was a Swede, of noble birth, a Count de Horn, handsome, elegant, rich, for he lived at Claridges, sported a magnificent coach and horses, and had two footmen dressed in splendid livery. He went everywhere. Society loved him, no rout or ball was complete without him. And he was intelligent too, for Angelica met him at Dr. Burney's house, and from then on he was a frequent visitor to her rooms, making a great impression on her by his charm and breeding.

Soon they became sufficiently intimate for him to confide in her his strange story. He said that, owing to political difficulties, he was not able to live in Sweden at the moment; he had enemies in high places who had spoken against him to the King, so that he could not be seen at Court. Even his life might be in danger, since the Swedish Ambassador in London intended to demand his person from the British Government. We have the story from Angelica's earliest biographer, Rossi, who says that her father told him that Horn, coming to her one day in great distress, said, "Only one hope is there of saving me, there is only one refuge for me, in your arms my angel. Give me your hand as my wife. Once the holy bond unites us, I am certain that the royal family, who love and esteem you, will not give up your husband, or allow him to be carried away to prison and certain death. If I escape now all will go well. I am innocent, and once I am free and in my own country I will defend myself. I will bring my accusers to shame and triumph over them, and it will be to you that I shall owe my happiness, my life. But there is not a moment to lose; either you make me your husband at once or I am a lost man."

Incredible as it may seem, Angelica believed him. In the strange world in which she lived, it was not impossible, for political and social intrigue were to be found everywhere. So was romantic love too, for that matter. The Count was pressing, ardent, flattering. No person of the English nobility, however they admired her person or her work, had honoured her with such an offer, though Lord John Cavendish, younger son of the Duke of Devonshire, is said to have been amongst her admirers. She may have loved Horn, she may well have pitied him; in any case she was tempted. By marrying him she would move in society in her own right, she would be done with patronage and be a patron herself, perhaps even an ambassadress. So she argued with herself, for she could consult no one, not even her father; for the Swede insisted on the strictest secrecy. Romance, ambition won, and on 22 November 1767 she met Horn at St. James's Church, Piccadilly, and gave him her hand as his wife.

The two witnesses were Annie Horne and Richard Horne, no one knows who they were. Rossi speaks of a subsequent second ceremony at a little Catholic church in the neighbourhood, probably that in Spanish Place where a priest blessed the union without witnesses or proper formalities and although it was still forbidden by law in England for a priest to marry two people of his own faith.

Once married Horn proceeded to take advantage of his wife's generosity. Three times he asked for loans of money, pleading necessity because his funds had not arrived. But when Angelica at last questioned this demand, he sent a priest to inform her father of the truth, considering that as his daughter's husband he should have the management of her affairs. Thunderstruck, the old man called his daughter in and questioned her. How could she have deceived him so? her unkindness would break his heart. That he, who lived only for her, should have lost her confidence, should have been treated less well than a stranger seemed inconceivable. Angelica, in tears, knelt before her father and implored his forgiveness, and assured him that in time he would love her husband, as she did, and forgive their fault.

Now the news of her marriage began to creep out and the Queen hearing of it, and Angelica being at Buckingham House one day, she questioned her. When she heard that the bridegroom was Count de Horn, she invited Angelica to present him to her. The Count being told this, made great difficulties, and he had all sorts of excuses. His baggage had not arrived from Sweden—he was waiting for a Swiss friend to bring it; he could not afford to equip himself properly, and much more of the same sort. Meanwhile he urged Angelica to leave London with him—still in secrecy—he must have trembled every time he met her lest his secret had leaked out.

For Horn was a complete impostor.

The marriage remains the one great and crucial blunder of Angelica's almost romantically successful career. The Greeks would have said that she had reason to dread fate because things had gone so well with her. The event is at once a thrilling highlight and a maddening hiatus in the narrative of her life. Did she love Horn? And did he love her or merely see in her a profitable investment, which would still pay good dividends no matter to whatever country in Europe he took her? Was the marriage ever consummated? Alternatively, was she only willing to marry him because he had already seduced her? Such a possibility cannot be ruled out but seems utterly unlikely in view of what we know of her character. She was a devout Catholic. But devout Catholics have been known to be seduced. Leaving religion aside, could she, with all her good sense and kindness of heart, have been betrayed by anything so shoddy as mere social ambition?

If even one of the contemporaries who had known the bogus Count—if Dr. Burney or his daughter Fanny—had left us so much as a few lines of comment upon him or upon Angelica's front to the world at this difficult time, we would have something, a little, a very little, to go upon. It was said, as we shall shortly see, that he was tried in the law courts for attempting to abduct or kidnap his "wife". But if this legal action was ever taken, where is the record of it? All we know is that the real Count arrived in London just about the time that Queen Charlotte was issuing her invitations to the bogus Count and naturally went to Court to pay his duty. When he was presented to the Queen, she congratulated him on his marriage to a gifted and charming bride. Astonished, the Count demanded to be put in touch with the man who had been impersonating him. Inquiries were set on foot, and one of Angelica's friends wrote to Horn challenging him to produce proof of his identity. A very weak reply followed which old Kauffmann showed to Angelica, who insisted that her husband should clear himself. Having no convincing reply, Horn took refuge in rage. He stormed at the two unhappy victims of his deceit, and rushed out of the house. Angelica was horrified! Was this the charming soft-spoken aristocrat she had married? In their bewildered misery, the two unhappy creatures tried to comfort each other, without much result, for they were caught in a mesh of dishonourable fact. Horn was the husband, and as such he did have undoubted rights over his wife, could command her to follow him, to help him and no one could prevent it legally. For three days they remained in this state of frozen terror, while one of their friends made real efforts to find out the truth of the sordid story. Then came a lawyer's clerk from Horn demanding instant submission from Angelica, or the alternative of a deed of separation and the payment of £500. By now Angelica was completely disillusioned, the separation was for her the only way out, but she very much disliked having to pay away so much of her hard earned money and she and her father proposed to take the matter to law. This would mean, however, long delays. Meanwhile the wretch, uncertain of the money, attempted to get hold of his wife by force. He hired some ruffians, had horses ready waiting and a boat which would carry her across the Channel. But the scheme somehow came to nothing, he was brought up before the Justices and charged with conspiracy; but again he was lucky, the sentence of imprisonment was annulled and he was discharged on his own recognisances. One asks oneself how was this fellow still at liberty; was there some very powerful influence behind him? It is a mystery.

Not so mysterious was the information which was now coming in. His real name was Brandt, but various cities on the Continent had known him by other names. And it was now established that he was the illegitimate son of the Count de Horn's father by a maidservant. He had been brought up in the Horn family, and so had intimate knowledge of them, their style, their possessions, and was thus able to impersonate the real Count. More important still, was the news that the scoundrel had married another woman who had lived with him at Hildesheim, where he gave himself out as a Colonel in the army of Frederick the Great. In half a dozen other towns he had lived with assumed names, in Hamburg, in the Hague, in Breslau; in Amsterdam he called himself Studerat, elsewhere Rosenkranz. In all of them he had practised fraud and imposture with varying success. Now as the evidence against him accumulated he became less demanding, and finally approached the Kauffmanns with an offer of a compromise. Angelica by this time only wished to see and hear the last of him and she accepted his demand for £300 in return for a document legally drawn up, in which he gave up his rights as a husband and left her free, promising never to hold any communication with her in future. In fact he left England and Angelica never saw him again. As is usual in such cases she had been overwhelmed with advice from her friends, many of whom wanted her to revenge herself on the villain who had so misused her. Fortunately her wiser and better self prevailed and her biographer Rossi tells us that she said, "If the Count has been guilty of bigamy and if his guilt is proved he will be sentenced to death, and if I should be the cause of this I should never know a moment's happiness. No, the spirit of revenge and anger dwells no longer in my breast, and although he injured me, and it may be has betrayed me, I leave his punishment in God's hands. Never speak his name to me again." A wise resolution, says Rossi, for what would have been the use of dragging her own name in the mud, to be the target for malicious comment from an all too willing press?

Brandt died in 1780, just at the time when her father had at last prevailed on her to appeal to Rome for an annulment of her marriage. It was in fact no marriage and could easily have been annulled, but his death put an end to the painful re-opening of the matter. One extraordinary and quite unacceptable explanation of the whole affair exists. Wurzbach Steinberg, Vagler, Angelica's foreign critics, all tell the same story—they do their best to put the blame on Sir Joshua Reynolds, of whom as an artist they had a very poor opinion. In fact they had a very poor opinion of English art in general and Steinberg writes thus of Angelica: "In England she was the centre of a frivolous circle, by whom she was again, as in Milan and Florence, led away, only with this difference; the rich aristocratic English were in a position to offer far greater temptations (especially to a luxurious temperament such as Angelica's) than the comparatively speaking, needy princes of Upper Italy and the Swiss Cantons. The Court, the nobility, the lords of the Parliament House, the owners of collections, and the leaders of fashion and talent poured their money into her hands. She herself was amazed at their generosity, but she did not reckon that her art was getting its death blow. England was the platform upon which she could exhibit her sentimental gods and goddesses. This prudish nation—a whited sepulchre so to speak of immodesty—applauded to the echo the delicacy which could handle doubtful subjects and yet know how to present them so as not to affront the feelings of society, hurt the prejudices of the British matron, or make the young English Miss blush. Art in fact was to be clothed in a sort of toilet luxury to please the taste of this eccentric nation, which found in Angelica an artist ready to gratify its ridiculous prejudices at the expense of the true principles and ideal of art itself."

So all these critics were only too pleased to find a stick with which to beat the hated protagonist of English art, Sir Joshua Reynolds. They asserted that he had engineered a plot to discredit Angelica, to get her married—this would be the aim of the suitors she had rejected—and would support any conspiracy which would bring this about. The absurdity of such an accusation would be apparent to anyone who knew the character of Sir Joshua at least, and even Fuseli, passionate as he was, would have been above such despicable behaviour. Moreover it presupposes that Reynolds and Fuseli were in the privileged position of knowing that Horn was a crook. In a town full of gossipy writers such as Horace Wapole and many others who adored above all a breath of scandal, such a plot would have been very shortly known and commented upon. In fact, not a word of such a story leaked out, and it can be entirely discredited; Angelica had jealous enemies certainly but they do not seem to have taken advantage of her sad plight, and how could they? She was guilty of nothing more than a misguided action; no blame could attach to her.

The end of this miserable episode was that, disillusioned and abased in her own eyes, she had to return to her easel and work doubly hard in order to recoup the financial loss she had sustained.

9

It would seem that the Royal Family showed their sympathy in quite a substantial way at this unfortunate
moment. The King sat for his portrait to her, and this royal
approval helped to bring more sitters so that in the year
1768 the Danish Prime Minister could write of her
"peculiar and womanly dignity which inspires the utmost
respect", and add his praise of the modest way in which she
had confronted her misfortune. A reference to her in his
letter as a St. Cecilia also shows that she was known as an
accomplished musician; her beautiful voice made her much
in demand at private parties. She was to have further proof
of the devotion of her friends as the year went on.

Although London at this time was full of painters with
first-class qualifications there was very little opportunity for
them to show their work other than in their own studios,
also London lacked a really adequate School of Art, where
students might work under the right conditions aided by
first-class masters. An academy started by Sir James
Thornhill earlier in the century had faded out with his
death; the next move was made by Angelica's friend
George Moser, who, as Farington relates, "made up a little
Academy for drawing from a living model by lamplight".
The report of this little Academy drew the attention of
Hogarth, and several other English artists, who visited it
and approved the plan proposed to Moser and the other
resident foreigners to unite with them in forming one on a
more extensive scale, which being agreed to, the Academy
in St. Martin's Lane was established, and continued to be
attended until the Royal Academy was founded.

But even Hogarth voiced criticism of the Academy which
he said with its low fees ran the risk of being simply a place
where boys with no sort of real talent could be kept off the

The Earl and Countess of Ely, with their two nieces. It was originally thought that Angelica had included herself in the portrait but Miss Anna Morris writes "The lady seated at the spinet is not Angelica Kauffmann, but my great, great, great, grandmother, Frances Monroe whose sister Dorothea, the famous Irish beauty stands at the spinet, apparently about to sing. The girls' parents died when they were young and the Earl and Countess took them to live with them at their family seat, Rathfarnham Castle." Courtesy of the National Gallery of Ireland, Dublin.

streets by anxious parents. And later a writer in the *London Tradesman* complained that there was little or no opportunity for an artist to be trained in England, for the Academy had few models to choose from and little or no teaching. "The subscribers set the figure, that is they place the man or woman in such attitude in the middle of the room as suits their fancy. He who sets the figure chooses what seat he likes, and all the rest take their places according as they stand on the list, and then proceed to drawing, every man according to his prospect of the figure."

Discontent with such efforts was in the air, and successive plans, more or less successful, were culminating in the sixties with the Exhibitions of the Free Society of Artists, which held its first Exhibition in Spring Gardens in 1761. In 1762 Dr. Samuel Johnson contributed a preface to the catalogue, in which he said: "The purpose of this exhibition is not to enrich the artist but to advance the art . . . but because it is seldom believed that money is got but for the love of money, we shall tell the use which we intend to make of our expected profits. Many artists of great abilities are unable to sell their works for their due price; to remove this inconvenience, an annual sale will be appointed, to which every man may send his works, and them, if he will, without his name. Those works will be reviewed by the committee that conduct the exhibition; a price will be set on every piece, and registered by the secretary; if the piece exposed is sold for more, the whole price shall be the artist's; but if the purchasers value it at less than the committee, the artist shall be paid the deficiency from the profits of the exhibition."

By 1765 the Society had 211 members, with such names as Reynolds, Gainsborough, Zoffany, West and many other distinguished artists, and it was granted a Charter. But differences arose and some members resigned, among them William Chambers, an architect who had been fortunate enough to obtain an introduction to the Princess Dowager of Wales from whom he received a commission to build the famous Pagoda at Kew. He had been a friend of Reynolds in their early days in Paris, but though ostensibly still

5—AK • •

friends they had developed a sort of love-hate relationship, for Reynolds had never succeeded in capturing royal favour. Chambers had taught architecture to the young Prince George who when he became King, gave him the position of Crown Architect, and later the office of Comptroller of Works and the first Surveyor General. The two men were playing a "great Game", says Derek Hudson, for Chambers was a classical architect with political talents and Reynolds an intellectual artist with a passion for art-theory and for broad generalisations. Now they came in close contact over the Foundation of the Academy of Art.

The battle began with the resignation of Chambers from the Society of Artists, the result of a struggle for its leadership in which he was defeated. But not entirely, for in November 1768 he and Benjamin West, Francis Cotes and George Moser drafted the constitution of a Royal Academy and carried it to the King, his pupil. It outlined a practical plan, asking him to found a school or academy of design for the use of students in the arts, and it also suggested that there should be an annual exhibition for the purpose of raising funds with which to finance the institution. Reynolds had taken no part in these deliberations, and indeed had been absent from London on a visit to France. In November he was back but still disinclined to take any part in the fratricidal battle between artists. Joseph Farington in his Diary gives an account of the events which terminated the struggle.

"West told Smirke and me that at a meeting at Wilton's where the subject of planning and forming the Royal Academy was discussed, Sir Wm. Chambers seemed inclined to be the President, but Penny (Edward Penny R.A.) was decided that a painter ought to be the President. It was then offered to Mr. Reynolds, afterwards Sir Joshua, though He had not attended any of those meetings which had been held at Mr. Wilton's. Mr. West was the person appointed to call on Sir Joshua to bring him to a meeting at Mr. Wilton's, where an offer of the Presidency was made to him, to which Mr. Reynolds replied that He desired to consult his friends Dr. Johnson and Mr. Burke. This hesitation was mentioned by Sir Willm. Chambers to the King, who from that time entertained a prejudice against Reynolds. For both Johnson and Burke were then disliked by the King, the latter particularly on political reasons." (They were both Whigs.)

However Reynolds must have been advised to accept the honour, for there is an entry in his notebook for 9 December, "Mr. Wilton's at 6"; and on 10 December the King signed the Instrument of Foundation of the Royal Academy. On 14 December the first meeting of the Academy took place in Pall Mall; Reynolds was formally elected to the chair, and signed the minutes with a typical flourish J. Reynolds President. It speaks well for the King that he could put his personal feelings on one side. Reynolds, with his tactful refusal to be embroiled, his undeviating devotion to art, and the best interests of artists and students, was the obvious man for the choice.

There were forty original members of the Academy with such names as Sandby, West, Bartolozzi, Cipriani, Wilson, Cosway, Zoffany, Nollekens, Dance and Hone among them. The extraordinary thing is that all these distinguished men should have included two women as founder Royal Academicians, and still more extraordinary that one of them should be Angelica Kauffmann, after only two years of residence in the country. It is proof of the position she had achieved, and still more proof that, if the influence of Reynolds counted for something in the appointment, he could not have been guilty of the treachery towards her of which he has been accused.

The Annual Register for 1768 includes a full account of the institution of the Academy, far too long to be given here. It is sufficient to say that its aims were to establish schools of design with living models. Nine leading academicians were to attend the schools in rotation to advise and instruct and professors were to be appointed to read a certain number of public lectures in the schools. A library would be brought together with books on all subjects pertaining to the arts and the admission to all these establishments would be free to bona fide students, proper salaries being paid to all concerned in the enterprise, the money to be drawn from the profits of various exhibitions, and the whole complex establishment would be under the personal patronage of His Majesty, "whose benevolence and generosity overflow in every action of life—hath allotted a considerable sum, annually to be distributed for the relief of indigent artists, and their distressed families". In fact the King was enormously proud of "his Academy" and took the greatest pleasure in hearing about its welfare.

All this development, and the honour paid her contributed to Angelica's recovery from her tragic experience, and her concentration on her painting helped to keep her mind from dwelling on it. For the pictures she was painting now demanded far more than portraiture; in the first place her reading became wide in search for subjects; Bernsdorff tells how he found her with Klopstock's *Messiah* in her hand, and Pope's *Homer* lay on the table beside her.

The first Exhibition of the Royal Academy opened at Messrs. Christie's Auction Rooms in Pall Mall and on 21 April Reynolds wrote in his note book, "12 The King's Levee", and on the opposite page, "Knighted at St. James's". It is said that Dr. Johnson that evening broke his rule and drank one glass of wine to the health of Sir Joshua Reynolds on the day on which he was knighted. It must have been a hilarious party.

On the 27th the *Advertiser* announced, "On Monday the Princess Dowager of Wales, and Yesterday His Majesty, accompanied by his Royal Highness the Duke of Gloucester, and the two Princes of Mecklenburg Strelitz visited the exhibition of the Royal Academy in Pall Mall, with which they expressed themselves highly satisfied." Angelica had sent four pictures, all of classical subjects: "Hector taking leave of Andromache", "Achilles Discovered by Ulysses amongst the Attendants of Deidamia", "Venus showing Aeneas and Achates the way to Carthage" and "Penelope taking down the bow of Ulysses for the trial of her suitors". The rooms were crowded, all rank and fashion were there, no one who was anyone could miss such an event, and the *Advertiser* says that the pictures which attracted most notice were three by Sir Joshua Reynolds, the "Regulus" of West and his "Venus lamenting the death of Adonis", and " 'Hector and Andromache' by Mrs. Angelica Kauffmann, an Italian young lady of uncommon genius and merit." It has been noted that, although both her conversation and the thoughts which she jotted down reveal her piety, Angelica preferred classical to Biblical subjects at this time, although later, after her return to Italy, she was to paint a few pictures with religious themes.

This picture was rather severely criticised by Count Bernsdorff, who says, "The defects in her method (grave ones I own) are in my opinion counterbalanced by the many beauties of thought and feeling with which her work is permeated. *Sensu tincta sunt.*[1] She shows great wisdom in her choice of a subject . . . Her composition is full of grace and the figures have the quiet dignity of the Greek models. Her women are most womanly and she conveys with much art the proper relation between the sexes, the dependence of the weaker on the stronger, which appeals very much to her masculine critics. It must be owned however that a little of this feebleness characterises her male personages. They are shy creatures; some of them look like girls in men's clothes, and it would be impossible for her to portray a villain. The colouring is very faulty, the background is monotonous, and a violet haze floats over the picture, which is detrimental to its beauty." All this did not prevent her selling it to Mr. Parker, one of her most faithful patrons. It is now at Saltram.

Zoffany painted a picture, "The Academicians studying the Naked Model", which nicely shows the implied difference between the masculine Academicians and the feminine ones, for the two ladies are only present in their portraits hanging on the wall. Leslie, in his *Life of Sir*

---

[1] Those things are steeped in feeling.

Joshua Reynolds, says, that "each face is an admirable likeness, and the peculiarity of every artist is caught and transferred to the canvas so as to strike every beholder". For instance, Cosway, the "Macaroni" painter,[1] is the only one beside Sir Joshua wearing a sword, and his gold lace and clouded cane, his inseparable regalia, single him out as a "glass of fashion". But Zoffany has certainly not done justice to Angelica in her portrait, for she looks hard-faced and severe.

Angelica was of course painting portraits during all this time and many small pictures in her favourite ovals. It was a form which appealed to her. She had painted a considerable number of self-portraits beginning with an early one at the age of thirteen. She had marked it on a piece of paper—"Mdccli ... in the thirteenth year of my age I painted it ... and my Father's and Fra Meuffer Contrafe Morbegno Valtlin."

The next was a portrait in the costume of the province painted in about the year 1762 or possibly when she was in Florence for the first time; then comes one in a very modish dress and with a Venetian colouring, probably shortly before her departure for England. Later came a portrait in a stylish Gainsborough hat, showing how well the prevailing mode suited her beauty.

Forgotten, or at least not often remembered, were the tragic events of the previous year; she had settled down to the system of persistent work which was really the basis of her life. And money began to pour in again, for she had increased her fees and got them, to the surprise of some of her colleagues. The critics too were a little kinder to Angelica than they had sometimes been; they were forced to acknowledge her obvious gifts as a portraitist. When in Rome she was influenced by the work of Pompeo Girolamo Batoni (1708–87) who has been called the inventor of "the grand tourist portrait", that is to say he painted his sitters—who were generally travellers, English or otherwise—against a background of picturesque antique ruins. Batoni painted three Popes and many princes and

---

[1] Macaroni was the name given to the exaggerated dandy of the time.

numerous examples of his work returned with their purchasers from Italy to adorn English country houses. Reynolds disparages Batoni in his Fourteenth Discourse, but then he was Reynolds's competitor for the custom of wealthy Englishmen. Batoni had been a favourite with the exiled Stuarts in Rome and his work had been deeply influenced by the neo-classicists around Cardinal Albani and his librarian, Winckelmann. Anthony M. Clark, in his very perceptive article in the *Bregenz Catalogue* of "Angelica Kauffmann and her Contemporaries" speaks especially of her two early pictures, the portrait drawing of Benjamin West and the *Bacchus and Ariadne* in the Bregenz Town Hall and says that the first shows strongly the influence of Mengs, the Bacchus clearly that of Batoni. Angelica was influenced by Batoni to the extent suggested, and she now rode to success on the crest of the same wave. "She excelled in portraits," says the *Allgemeine Biographie*, and the *Biographie Universelle* remarked the elegance of her draperies "which are never confused, and the attitude is always well chosen, although her figures are often wanting in strength of colour and vigour of touch".

It was not only her portraits which sold, but her large historical canvases too, which adorn today such houses as Saltram, Burghley, Harewood and many, many others. She suited the fashion for mythology, and the learned Blue Stockings who gathered to discuss the finer points of the Greek poets. They even met in the country houses in spite of the weather, which differed very little from what we have today. Walpole noted that on 15 June 1768, "the deluge began here and then rained for eight and forty hours without stopping. My poor hay has not a dry thread to its back, I have had a fire these three days. In short every summer one lives in a state of mutiny and murmur, and I have found the reason. It is because we will affect to have a summer and we have no title to any such thing. Our poets learned their trade from the Romans ... they talk of purling streams, shady groves and cooling breezes, and we get sore throats and agues with attempting to realise these visions."

Angelica for the most part stayed in town, with an occasional visit to a country house where she was commissioned. Such was Harewood House, in Yorkshire, where she designed the ceiling of the state gallery and the beautiful pictures inset in its frieze.

In the year 1770 Angelica received a commission which relates her most intimately with our own time. As we enter Burlington House to view the exhibitions there, the first pictures which meet us, if we lift our eyes to them, are the four oval paintings by her representing Composition, Invention, Design and Colouring. In 1770 each Academician, when he received his diploma, was required to give to the Academy a representative work, but this being two years after the Foundation, the Collection had no works by the forty original members. To make up the number, other works by the missing ones were added and Angelica among them contributed these pictures. They were originally placed in the ceiling of the Council at Somerset House but when the Royal Academy moved to Burlington House they were taken down and hung in the vestibule where they can now be seen.

The demand for reproduction of her most successful paintings was enormous and the happy chance which had brought her into touch with the engraver William Ryland served this demand. His colour plates have a softness and delicacy of touch which explain their deservedly high reputation, but his story is a tragic one. He was one of seven sons of a copperplate printer who lived in Newgate Street near the Old Bailey. After being apprenticed to Ravanet he was given the opportunity to go to Paris where he studied design under Le Bas. After a five-year stay in France he returned to England where he soon made the acquaintance of Angelica whose fame he helped to spread by his skill as an engraver. Ryland had great charm and Angelica is supposed to have flirted with him, for he had not informed her that he was a married man and an ex-bankrupt. He delighted in her patronage and called her "his ministering angel", and she had every reason to be grateful to him. When, however, it was discovered that he had not only a wife but also a mistress and an illegitimate child, she withdrew her patronage and he was soon in financial difficulties once more. Presently he disappeared and a handbill was distributed offering a reward of three hundred pounds for his discovery. He was wanted on a charge of forgery, committed it was said for the sake of his mistress and her little child. He was caught, tried on what many consider very shaky evidence, found guilty and duly hanged. Prejudice is said to have operated against him for he was a Catholic and anti-Romanist feeling ran high, culminating in the No-Popery Riots of 1780.

He had paid Angelica extravagant attention and the disclosure of his marriage and liaison may have mortified her deeply. But he was by no means the only engraver at that time to secure the copyright of her designs. Bartolozzi, Burke and Boydell, McArdle in Dublin, Delabre and Jacques Clerck in Vienna and innumerable others found in her pictures a fertile source for their work. Her pictures inspired J. J. Spängler, a Swiss like herself, to make three wonderful groups of Derby biscuit porcelain. And they furnish Worcester, Derby and Swansea with hundreds of designs. Even the Sèvres and Meissen factories made use of her work. These elegant and delicate reproductions so prized in their day have long been out of fashion. But it is likely that the enterprising explorer of dusty antique shops or forgotten rooms in old houses, will be rewarded by small but perfect works of art. She was a competent engraver and etcher herself. She had made an excellent etching of her portrait of Winckelmann for the writer. She gave one copy of this etching to her friend Count Bernsdorff before he left London with the King of Denmark. "Angelica has given me a charming present of some etchings of her own doing," he wrote, "which are not to be had in any print shop. Amongst them I am particularly pleased with a likeness of our Winckelmann. He sits at this desk, his pen in his hand, searching with his eagle eye to discover in Apollo's nose, or the torso of Hercules, where lay their contempt for the Gods."

10

Angelica had successfully surmounted her matrimonial and financial troubles; she was admired, courted, and successful, and it was in this state that she accepted the invitation of Lord Townsend, the Viceroy, to pay a visit to Ireland. The journey to Ireland in those days was almost as hazardous and uncomfortable as that from the Continent, but whatever sea-sickness Angelica endured would have been recompensed by the beauty of the approach to Dublin through its wonderful bay, only to be compared to that of Naples. The city too presented such an agreeable air that she must have felt immediately at home.

We do not know where she was lodged but it was surely in the centre of a town which was becoming yearly finer and more splendid. Although it was not until 1774 that an Act of Parliament provided for the increased clearing away of the narrow streets and the opening of public avenues, and for new paving, people like her client, the Hon. David Latouche, already inhabited fine houses like his in St. Stephen's Green, and Lord Charlemont's in Palace Row. This magnificent nobleman filled his mansion with treasures brought back from his Grand Tours. Lord Charlemont had been painted in Rome by Batoni and the inventory of his pictures, statuary, books, would fill volumes. Many of these houses may still be seen, and an idea of the extent of the improvements lies still in the broad streets and noble squares of Dublin. North Great George's Street, Gardiner Street, Granby Street and Palace Row formed a Square with the garden of the Lying-in Hospital in the centre and the Rotunda at its east end. It bore then the name of Rutland Square from that of the Duke who contributed largely to its formation.

But all their splendour paled before that of the Viceroy

and Castle which dominated the City and was the seat of Government. It dated from 1215 but had been modernised and most of the old buildings swept away; deplorable in a sense, but practical, for besides being the habitation of the King's representative, it now housed the arsenal and 40,000 soldiers. Here Lord Townsend kept a Court which vied in elegance and gaiety with anything London could show. The latest French fashion in gowns and hair styles bedecked the ladies, and the games played by Marie Antoinette and her friends in their retreat at Trianon were imported too. One was the Cutchacutchoo, a sort of blind-man's-buff, but even more rowdy, in which lords and ladies hopped about, but in a sitting posture, and great was the merriment when one belle was capsized by a heavier rival.

It is doubtful whether Angelica saw much of these revels however; she would be much too busy fulfilling the numerous commissions with which she had come supplied. But we know that she visited and decorated the magnificent seat of the Marquis of Ely at Rathfarnham Castle and painted the grandee himself with his Marchioness. Included in the picture are the lovely Dolly Monroe, and her sister Frances leaning over a spinet, pointing to music which she evidently knows well.[1] The noble Lord presents a pompous aspect to the world, and his Lady followed by the little negro page bearing the coronet seems to insist in rather a snobbish way on their magnificence. But the exquisite Monroe, a niece of Lady Ely, gives the lie to any suggestion of stiff pretentiousness, and the picture

1 This picture was thought to contain Angelica seated at the harpsichord but the author has recently received a letter from a descendant of the Munro family which states: "The lady seated at the spinet is not as indicated by the notice below Angelica Kauffmann herself but my great great great grandmother Frances Munroe [sic] (maiden name) whose sister Dorothea (or Dolly) Munroe, the famous Irish beauty, stands apparently about to sing. They were nieces of Lord and Lady Ely (Loftus, my father's side of the family, who stand on the right). The girl's parents having died when they were young, the Countess took them to live with them at their family seat Rathfarnham Castle, built in 1500 by a Marquess of Ely." It has been pointed out that it would have been audacious of the artist to include herself in the family group; what more natural than to include Frances with her sister.

hangs now in a place of honour in the National Gallery in Dublin. We are told that Lord Townsend pretended to Lady Ely that he was much enamoured of her niece—he would have been an excellent match—and kept up the pretence until the Marchioness had prevailed on her lord to give him his vote, when he came out in his true colours and married a Miss Montgomery, greatly to Lady Ely's displeasure. Dublin gossip had it that it was Ely himself who was really in love with Dolly, an aspect of the affair which, if true, must have displeased his wife even more.

Angelica was a celebrity and entertained on all sides. Mr. Latouche had a fine seat at Marley, at no great distance from the town where she would have a ravishing view of the encircling mountains, and the beautiful gardens with their running streams and fountains. And although she did no decorations there, she must have visited Castletown, admired as the finest house in all Ireland. It belonged to the Right Hon. Thomas Connolly, a man of immense wealth, and lay in a magnificent park. Ireland was at this time full of men who could afford to indulge themselves like their English counterparts in building and embellishing their estates with spacious parks and gardens. Around them clustered the hovels of the Irish, bereft of such things as schools, medical care or any means of even tolerable living.

She painted Lady Caroline Damer at Emo Park, and Lord Ferrard and his son at Antrim Castle; also a picture called "The Death of Sylvia's Stag" for Justice Downes of the Queen's Bench. In Ireland are many houses and rooms supposed to have been decorated by her, so many in fact that she would have to have been an accomplished athlete and to have worked night and day during her six months' stay to have done them all. Some, however, are completely authenticated. And Rossi, who is to be trusted, says that she prepared sketches for a vast amount of work which she promised to complete on her return to England.

The spring of 1772 saw her back in London after her visit, which had been both artistically and socially a triumph. She arrived in a town where it seemed that the majority of the people she knew paid little attention to anything other than amusement and the spending of money. Already in 1770 Horace Walpole had written to his friend Sir Horace Mann: "What do you think of the new winter Ranelagh erecting in Oxford Street at the expense of sixty-thousand pounds." This was the Pantheon, and he goes on to expatiate on the extravagance of the times and to say that "the new bank including the value of the ground and the houses demolished to make room for it will cost three-hundred thousand . . . I have touched before on the incredible profusion of our young men of fashion. I know a younger brother who literally gives a flower woman a guinea every morning for the nosegay in his buttonhole. We have at present three Exhibitions. One West, who paints history in the taste of Poussin, gets three-hundred pounds for a piece not too large to hang over a chimney . . . The rage to see these exhibitions is so great that sometimes one cannot pass through the streets where they are. Another rage is for prints of English portraits. I have been collecting them for thirty years and originally never gave for a mezzotint above one or two shillings. The lowest are now a crown, most from half-a-guinea to a guinea." It is the cry of the collector throughout the ages, but it explains why the artists and their engravers could live well.

By 1772 the Pantheon was almost ready, it was to cost fifty thousand pounds, its glory was amazing; with its pillars of artificial marble, its gilded and painted ceilings and its dome resembling its Roman prototype, it astonished all who saw it. Such splendour, such luxury! Monsieur de Guines, the French Ambassador said to Walpole, "Ce n'est qu'à Londres qu'on peut faire tout cela."[1] This from a man familiar with Versailles was praise indeed. But Walpole had more to say to his friend than these gossipy letters; his disquiet at events in France and America was equalled by his fears of riots in the streets of London, and his horror at the insurrection in Ireland where four thousand men, calling themselves Hearts of Steel, rose against their landlord Lord Donegal. They were driven off

[1] "It is only in London that one could achieve all that."

their land because they could not pay hard fines for not renewing their leases. Sixteen hundred horse and infantry were sent in against them.

As a contrast to this was the long-awaited opening of the Pantheon; everyone was there, including Mrs. Delany, who describes the brilliant masquerade but says the robbers in the High Street created many panics. "But pleasure will conquer all fears and men on horseback with a pistol will at last grow so familiar as to be no more regarded than the turnpike which makes you pay for your passage."

Nothing, neither the dangers of footpads nor the temptations of pleasure could stop Angelica painting, and in 1772 she sent five pictures to the Royal Academy. To this period also belong some of her best etchings, in particular "Die Haarflecherin" (The woman with plaited hair) 1765; "L'allegro" and "Il Pensieroso" 1779; and more especially "St. Peter rebuking his brother Apostle St. Paul," after Guido's picture in the Casa Sempiere in Bologna. Angelica etched this subject three times, and the one executed in 1772 is adjudged to be the best.

Angelica was now thirty-one childhood and youth had been left behind, together with their early successes she was fully aware of her powers, and under the admiration and approval which her work aroused her art expanded still more freely. To be mentioned only in the context of the most eminent painters of the time, was certainly an achievement for the little girl from the Grisons. Although she had been so much helped by Reynolds, she had not adopted his style; rather it was the great painter who had followed the neo-classical mode so far that he made the concession of painting his women sitters in pseudo-classical attire, and gave them the names of heroines of ancient history. Angelica now began even more ambitious works on mythological and historical themes and 1773 saw five of her canvases in the spring Academy.

In this year too a further compliment was paid to her. Reynolds had suggested that the Chapel of Old Somerset House be decorated by a number of artists; but in

October a much more ambitious project was contemplated, no less than to decorate the interior of St. Paul's in order, in the words of the Dean and Chapter, "To make this cathedral one of the finest structures in the world". They applied to the body of Royal Academicians for their superintendence and support. There was a meeting of the whole body at Somerset House, when it was resolved that six members should be appointed to carry out the plan, each beginning with painting a picture according to the design which should be agreed upon. The names of the six were Mrs. Angelica Kauffmann, Sir Joshua Reynolds, Sig. Cipriani, Mr. West, Mr. Dance and Mr. Barry. Her sex gave her precedence in this distinguished list and is also an indication of her eminence. But the appointment poses certain questions. How came it that she, a Roman Catholic, should be asked to decorate a Protestant place of worship; and even if she were asked, how could she reconcile it with her conscience? The times were far from ecumenical. A papist to decorate St. Paul's? To these questions there is no answer, and in the event her feelings were not strained, for the project came to nothing, through the intervention of Dr. Terrick, the Bishop of London. He was determined that while he lived the doors of the Metropolitan Church should never be opened for the introduction of Popery; he had his way and the worshippers in the Cathedral were not offended by graven—or painted—images!

In the year 1774 another flattering scheme in which Angelica's name also appeared was mooted. A number of artists were invited to decorate the great Room of the Society of Arts in the Adelphi. The names are much the same as in the previous list with the addition of Mortimer, Wright, Romney and Barry. She and seven others were to paint History. Romney and Penny were to paint Allegory. All of them declined to do the work, but some three years afterwards Barry offered to do the work himself and his offer was accepted. His decorations may be seen today in the Society's rooms in John Street, Adelphi, and a very strange sight they are.

In 1775, there were even more pictures. Eleven in all were despatched to the Academy. Some of her colleagues were put out because so many works were sent by one painter. Angelica was not inclined to take any notice of their complaints, but her father took the matter more seriously; she was being treated unfairly, he said, when four or five of them were not hung. He persuaded Angelica to complain to Reynolds; the absent pictures were brought back; thus four of them do not appear in the catalogue itself, but in the list of omitted pictures on page 34. By this time, the impact of her originality had lessened; many other painters were copying her choice of subjects, particularly those from the Middle Ages and English history. Also a certain monotony in the structure of her pictures begins to creep in. We come to expect the head inclined gracefully, the cheek resting on the hand in an elegiac mood, and also a certain disposal of the draperies which occurs again and again. But, as a portraitist, her skill never wavered and one can find little fault with either her masculine or her feminine subjects.

...thaniel Hone's "The Conjuror". For the sketch of the over-painted section, see illustration ... 52 in the black and white section. Courtesy of the National Gallery of Ireland, Dublin.

11

In this year, 1775, amongst the pictures sent to the Academy Exhibition was one which occasioned an art-world scandal in which Angelica figured. It was by Nathaniel Hone, a painter in enamel, of some eminence, but, we are told, a grudging and jealous man. He had produced a large canvas depicting a Sorcerer and entitled "The Pictorial Conjuror, Displaying the whole art of Optical Deception". It showed an old man in a gown, holding a wand in his hand summoning up engravings of old masters, while in the background floated the outline of St. Paul's Cathedral, with many naked figures dancing in front of it, of which one was that of a woman wearing high black boots. Leaning on the old man's knee was a childish figure painted in the style of Sir Joshua's paintings of children. The implication was barefaced, that Reynolds was a plagiarist; but, strange to say, the viewing committee of the Academy passed it and the picture was hung.

A great deal was to follow. Soon it was being said that one of the nude figures represented Angelica. It was an outrage, declared her friends. Sir William Chambers and other members of the Academy visited Hone in his studio and informed him that there was a rumour abroad that he had intended an insult to a distinguished artist, which they much regretted. Mr. Hone expressed himself as surprised and assured them that no insult was intended. His eloquence was such that they were "so obliging to do him the justice to say they had carefully looked at the figures and would clear him of the supposition of there being any woman figure; that they were well assured they were intended to mean the opposite sex". Hone declared that he was ready to erase the figure in question from the canvas

6—AK * *

immediately and he even offered to give the figures beards. On the next day he went to Angelica's house to assure her further that he had never meant to hurt her, nothing could be further from his mind. But she refused to see him, and another call met with the same result. Whereupon he wrote to her:

"Madam: The evening before last I was not a little surprised at a deputation from the Council of the Academy, acquainting me that you were most prodigiously displeased at my making a naked figure in my picture of the Conjuror now at the Royal Academy representing your person. I immediately perceived some busy meddler, to say no worse, had imposed this extravagant lie, of whose making God knows, upon your understanding. To convince you, Madam, that your figure in that composition was the farthest from my thoughts, I now declare I never at any time saw your works but with the greatest pleasure and that respect due to a lady that I esteem as the first of her sex in painting, and the loveliest of women in person. Envy and detraction must have worked strangely, for yesterday morning some more gentlemen from the Academy assured me that your uneasiness was very great. I assured them I could so far alter the figure that it would be impossible to suppose it a woman, though they cleared me of such a supposition themselves, as they understood it to be a male figure, and that I could put a beard on it, or dress it to satisfy you and them ... I am, Madam, your obedient humble servant.

N. Hone."

This rings true and quite possibly was true, because the fact of the matter is that the whole sting of the picture was directed against Reynolds and not against Angelica at all. It is just possible that Hone included a side-blow against the latter as the known friend of Reynolds and it is even possible that the booted female figure was an allusion to the extraordinary aberrative and fetishistic drawings of

Angelica's other friend Henry Fuseli, which have been kept
from the public view and in which nudity and fetishism are
linked in a rather outrageous fashion. But this is unlikely.
The plain truth is that neither Reynolds himself nor the
members of the Academy could demean themselves by
admitting that a direct attack had been made upon their
President. It would have been beneath their dignity to do
so. A different excuse had to be found and this was the
brilliant suggestion from some quarter that an honoured
lady-Academician had been slandered. In this way,
Reynolds's name could be left out of the whole business.

To Hone's letter Angelica replied, perhaps at the insti-
gation of her father who may have believed that a libel upon
his daughter really was intended and that only the complete
removal of the picture from the exhibition could be an
adequate apology:

> "Sir: I should have answered you immediately, but I was
> engaged in business. I cannot conceive why several gentle-
> men, who have never before deceived me, should con-
> spire to do it at this time, and if they themselves were
> deceived, you cannot wonder that others should be
> deceived also, and take for satyr (satire) that which you
> say was not intended. I was actuated, not only by my
> particular feelings, but a respect for the arts and artists,
> and persuade myself that you cannot think it a great
> sacrifice to remove a picture, that had even raised
> suspicion of disrespect to any person who never wished
> to offend you.
>
> I am, Sir,
>
> > Your humble servant,
> > Angelica Kauffmann.
> > To Nathaniel Hone Esq.
> > Pall Mall."

On Tuesday, 13 April, she sent another letter, in which
she said that she had received a visit from Sir William
Chambers and others who sought to persuade her to allow
the picture to remain; they seemed to suggest that she

would in so doing earn their respect, to which she replied
that she would admire their behaviour much more if they
sought to protect the honour of the sex they were supposed
to admire. She continued:

"If you fear the loss of a member who has not rendered
the respect which is due to my sex, I hope for the
freedom to tender to you the pleasure of retaining that
member and to allow a person who has never deserved to
be made ridiculous by him or by you to withdraw.

"I ask for permission to express my admiration for the
Society, and hope that it will always treasure my own
honour—I have only one wish—to withdraw my own
pictures, if this picture is exhibited.

I am your humble servant gentlemen.

Golden Square.
Tuesday Morning."

If she was fighting Reynolds's battle she was certainly doing valiant service to her old friend, but it
looks as though she really did believe that an insult
had been intended to her for on the same day she wrote to
Hone:

"Sir: The information which was brought to me about
the questionable picture came from more than one
person—my father has, on my request, seen it and
confirms what had been told me before—at the same
time as he was given to understand that if the figure of
the sitting woman with the trumpet were removed I
would be satisfied—but this figure must be absolutely
removed and no other be substituted—otherwise I hold
to my first decision, to retire my own pictures.

I have the honour, Sir, to be your humble servant,

Angelica Kauffmann
Tuesday."

It was too late for this solution. On the evening of the
same day, Mr. Hone received, to his amazement and disap-
pointment, a letter from the secretary of the Academy, as
follows:

"Sir:

I am desired to inform you that a vote of the Council has been taken and that the result is negative. You are therefore asked to remove your picture as soon as it is possible. I am Sir your obedient and humble servant.

F. M. M. Newton
Exhibition Room Pall Mall Tuesday evening.
N. Hone Esq."

Hone had already decided, if the verdict should go against him, to arrange an exhibition of his work, the centre piece of which should be "The Conjuror". He therefore published a legal document in which he swore that since he had been suspected of having painted a figure which resembled Mrs. Angelica Kauffmann, or any other lady, he had given the clearest assurance to Sir William Chambers and three other gentlemen who came to him to inquire into the matter, and at the same time he had promised that the figure which had given offence would be removed. On 2 May 1775, the picture, with other works was duly exhibited opposite Old Slaughter House at the top end of St. Martin's Lane, and Hone presented free copies of his "Apology to the Public" to all who attended. The picture then disappeared for some years, appearing in the sale of Hone's belongings in March 1785, and again in sales in 1790 and 1821, until in 1944 it appeared in Christies' salerooms. It was bought in 1967 by the National Gallery of Ireland where it now hangs, and at that point its history seemed ended. X-rays had indeed shown that beneath the overpainting of a group of gentlemen sitting round a table and contemplating St. Paul's, there were dimly to be seen the controversial "naked figures, and among them, clearly distinguishable, the lady in the black boots".

There was more to come. Quite unexpectedly various galleries received letters stating that, somewhere in central Brazil, there was to be had an original sketch by Hone for the picture. No notice was taken of such a far-fetched offer, until one day in August 1967 there arrived at the Tate

Gallery three charming young Brazilians with the sketch![1]
They brought not only the sketch but a copy of the
catalogue of Hone's exhibition hitherto unobtainable. After
prolonged bargaining, the gallery became the owner of the
sketch and all the accompanying documents, a cutting from
a news sheet of the time, Hone's patent as Lieutenant of the
III Infantry Regiment of 9 December 1763, and a cutting
from the *Daily Telegraph* of 1929 concerning the sale of one
of Hone's portraits. This was one of those moments for
which every collector longs, a pipedream that hardly ever
comes true.

Was Hone guilty of deliberate malice and, if so, what
were his motives in pillorying a woman colleague who had
done him no harm? The sketch shows that in truth the
naked women were there and, as well, the significance of a
pictured St. Paul's in the background had obvious reference
to the abortive attempt at decoration in which she as well as
Reynolds would have participated and which went up in the
smoke which shadows the figures. It is obvious that the latter
was the main target for Hone's satire, as even the news
sheets of the day show. The *London Evening Post* of 4 May
1775, and the *Public Advertiser* of 12, 15 and 20 May had
articles pointing this out clearly. And Mr. Martin Butlin in
his admirable article in the Catalogue of the Exhibition in
Bregenz of 1968 "Angelica Kauffmann and her
Contemporaries", goes at some length into the sources of
the pictures strewn around the Conjuror. The present
writer has a strong suspicion, for which there is however no
actual proof, that Angelica was called in by her eminent
friend in collusion over the affair. It would have been out of
the question that the President of the Royal Academy
should have entered the lists on his own behalf; he therefore
with the painter's own consent used her as a "front" for
having the picture removed. They were intimate friends,
they must have discussed the whole case closely and

---

[1] The name of the leader was Florinda Ferreira dos Santos and it is
probable they had bought the sketch from the original Brazilian owner
outright though it was just possible they were acting as his agents.

come to the conclusion that this would be the best way to beat off a scurrilous attack.

In striving to discredit both Reynolds and Angelica Hone did nothing but discredit himself; he was unpopular and now became even more so. Smith, in his life of Nollekens, tells of a subsequent incident, how "one morning a tall, upright, large man, with a broad brimmed hat, and a lapelled coat buttoned up to his stock, with measured and stately steps, entered the studio and walked up to Mr. Nollekens, who was then modelling a bust of Sir Eyre Coote, and full of self importance saluted him with, 'Joseph Nollekens Esq. R.A., how do you do?' Nollekens, who never liked him replied, 'Well now I suppose you've come to get me to join you at the Academy tonight, against Sir Joshua, but you're very much mistaken, and I can tell you more, I never will join you in anything you propose: you are always running your rigs against Sir Joshua; and you may say what you please, but I have never had any opinion of you since you painted that picture of the Conjuror, as you called it. I don't wonder they turned you out of the Academy. And pray what business had you to bring Angelica into it? You know it was your intention to ridicule her, whatever you or your printed paper and your affidavits may say: however you may depend on it she won't forget it, if Sir Joshua does.'"

There is no evidence that Angelica ever tried to take revenge on the man who had so meanly affronted her, but the affair had once more given her name an unenviable notoriety.

12

The unsavoury Hone affair was over and the year 1776
opened with the usual bad weather and Angelica hard at
work on her pictures for the next Academy Exhibition. A
new sensation had gripped the fickle society on which
Angelica was so largely dependent.

The main topic of conversation was the trial of the
Duchess of Kingston, which had been hanging fire for some
time and for which the town had been waiting with mount-
ing excitement. This lady, formerly the beautiful Miss
Chudleigh, of dubious fame, was on trial in Westminster
Hall before the House of Peers, for marrying the
Duke of Kingston during the lifetime of her first husband,
Augustus Earl of Bristol. It must have been difficult at
times for ladies to remember in whose bed they were
sleeping. "A quarter of our peeresses will have been the
wives of half our Peers," commented Walpole. Lord
Maynard had recently married the notorious Nancy
Parsons, who charms us in Reynolds's portrait in the
National Gallery. She had been kept by the Dukes of
Grafton, Dorset, etc. He was waiting till Lady Derby was
divorced and so would not marry her. Derby did; and
almost immediately Maynard wanted her back. Walpole's
friend, Lady Ossory, was the divorced wife of the Duke of
Grafton.

For Angelica they were all the same, unless she painted
them. The whole world of London was so occupied with
this trial, of which Walpole said with justice that it would all
be forgotten in two hundred years, that they had hardly
time to think of the opening of the Royal Academy exhibition on 21 April, to which exhibition Angelica sent five
pictures. It is noticeable that her favourite subjects are
mainly those where a gentle and devoted woman is either

mourning, or imploring, or engaged in some other deeply feminine occupation. She avoided heroic and manly subjects. Perhaps she was conscious of her own deficiency as others were, for now was the time when Fuseli began to criticise her. "Germans," he said, "call her the 'Paintress of the Soul'; her male and female figures never vary in form, feature or expression from the favourite ideal in her own mind. Her heroes are all the man to whom she thought she could have submitted, though him, perhaps, she never found. Her heroines are herself, and while suavity of countenance and alluring graces shall be able to divert the general eye from the sterner demands of character and expression, she can never fail to please." A sour comment from a disappointed lover but with truth in it. This estimate of her character from a man who knew her very well and intimately is very enlightening. It would seem that in her youth she had been the type who enjoys leading a man on, but never to the ultimate end of a love affair. The French call it *allumeuse* while the English have a somewhat coarser name for it. In her affair with Horn, she had been taken in by her desire for nobility, to be the equal in rank with her patrons. Now she was older, and perhaps wiser, and her really good nature, her innate sweetness and purity began to play a larger part in her development.

Peter Pindar, in his *Odes to Royal Academicians* gives blunt expression to the contention that all the heroes in her pictures were emasculated:

> Angelica my plaudits gains,
> Her Art so sweetly canvas stains
> Her Dames, so gracious, give me such delight
> But, were she married to such gentle Males
> As figure in her painted tales
> I fear she'd find a stupid wedding night.

But her popularity continued. So many people found their way to her elegant house in Golden Square that she now figured as one of the most outstanding figures in London life. She had probably established the habit of receiving on Sunday, for we shall see that this was continued in Rome.

Criticism, however, was not lacking. Farington records in his diary that Hoppner, Smirke and Barry at tea with him were discussing the various merits of artists, and Hoppner, himself a leading portraitist, dwelt much on the "bad taste which prevails in this country, (so) that the silly poetry of Della Cruscan and the works of Angelica Kauffmann in painting have captivated the public so as to corrupt the taste. I could not join him in the length he went on this subject." One is reminded over and over again that half her success was due to her temperamental response to the taste of her time: the other half of her appeal lay in the delicacy of her colouring. A certain simplicity in her harmonious grouping still holds its charm for us as it did for her contemporaries.

The year 1779 opened with one of the worst storms England had ever experienced; hardly a London house escaped damage. In February Garrick died, and was buried with great ceremony in Westminster Abbey. Angelica must have been there, and must have remembered with a sense of loss her first English sitter, and his playful comment. For the April Exhibition that year, she sent in as usual an impressive number of works, seven in all. Her manner exactly suited the houses which the Brothers Adam and Wyatt and others were building at this time. The neo-classical style, founded on the Pompeian interior, fitted well into the great country and town houses, with their large rooms which needed just this rich fastidious amplification. One of the foremost of these decorators was the Venetian painter Antonio Pietro Zucchi, who had met Robert Adam in Italy and whose brother Giuseppe accompanied Adam in 1757 on their great expedition to Spalato (Split) in Dalmatia to measure the magnificent palace of the Emperor Diocletian. It was Zucchi who engraved many of the plates which Adam issued to illustrate the result of his findings—published as *The Ruins of the Palace of the Emperor Diocletian at Spalato in Dalmatia*. Antonio and his brother were from Venice. They had come to England in middle life and Antonio was elected a member of the Academy a year after its foundation, which shows the esteem in which he was then held. He has been described as "a proud, reserved man, exceedingly upright and very highly respected", and his paintings of Piranesi-like ruins reveal his talent. In the compositions which decorate the dining room of Kedleston Hall, near Derby, Zucchi competes with painters like Claude Lorain, Romanelli, Snyders and Zuccarelli.

The work of the brothers Adam, who were responsible for many of the most beautiful of the great mansions which are still the pride of our town and countryside, degenerated presently into decorative effects which allowed Walpole to call it "Larded and embroidered and pomponned with shreds and remnants, and clinquant like all the harlequinades which never let the eye repose a moment". Such is the red drawing room at Syon House long attributed to Angelica but now known to have been by Cipriani. And such are many of their other decorations. But at the time we are speaking of, these decorations were much more chaste, and Angelica was much in demand as a designer and often as the executor of the work. And yet, it is difficult to establish which of the houses attributed to her she really did work in, for she left few records. Sir John Soames stated that Robert Adam employed, as well as Angelica, Clarisseau, Hamilton and Zucchi. For example, the ceiling of the vestibule at Kenwood, which has always been regarded as hers, is now stated to be by Biagio Rebecca; but the bill for Zucchi's work shows that he also was busy there. He sets exactly the subjects for his decorations, each of them *tirée de l'antique*, and their size. The *Mémoire de Mr. Zucchi pour les tableaux peints pour Son Excellence My Lord Mansfield* lists the items and their individual price. He painted too the dining room ceiling in Garrick's house at No. 3 Adelphi Terrace, next door to that of Adam at No. 4. The paintings at Chandos House are commonly supposed to be by Angelica and to bear her signature, and while she was in Ireland she painted some houses, notably that of Mr. Latouche at 52 St. Stephen's Green, and a beautiful small boudoir at Rathfarnham Castle, then the seat of the Marquis of Ely. At Abbeyville, Malahide, in County Dublin, there are three lovely panels in the ballroom, which are hers. But with so much of her work everywhere there are no records, and as it would have been physically impossible for her to have accomplished such a mountain of commissions in the six months she was there, it is possible that she made the designs which were carried out by other artists.

When we crane our necks to see the elaborate paintings with which the ceilings of the palaces of the time were decorated we ask ourselves how such a frail woman could have supported the strain. The answer is that like many of her colleagues, she painted the designs on specially prepared paper, which was afterwards pasted on the walls and ceilings. Robert Adam has left the record of doors in Derby House, Grosvenor Square, with panels "beautifully painted by Zucchi on Papier Maché and so highly japanned as to resemble glass". The panels on the sideboard and the two great urns in the dining room at Saltram are by Angelica and must have been pasted on in just this way.

In 1778 had come the important commission to decorate the ceiling of the new lecture rooms at Somerset House with four panels for which she was offered the sum of one hundred pounds. The Account Ledgers show the listing of "Work done by sundry Persons for the Right Honourable the Lords Commissioners of His Majesty's Treasury for the new offices at Somerset House under the direction of Sir William Chambers", and have this entry:

> To Angelica Kauffmann
> For painting 4 Pictures for the ceiling of ⎫
> the Lecture Room, to the Roy. Academy ⎬ £100.0.0
>   ⎭

And her receipt is in existence:

> Recd. June 22 1780 of the Lords of the Treasury, by the hands of Sr. Wm Chambers, the sum of one hundred pounds, being in full for four pictures painted for a ceiling in the Royal Academy at Somerset House.
> £100   by me Angelica Kauffmann.

In the year 1780, Angelica received good news which, if it had come earlier, might have changed her whole life.

Brandt was dead, she was a free woman once more. But free
for what? She was now thirty-nine, not a young woman any
longer, and if a friend described her as "sad and ailing" it is
not to be wondered at. But there were still triumphant
moments and one of them must have been the opening of
the new rooms of the Royal Academy at Somerset House in
May. There she could see her panels in a setting "finished
in perfect taste", says Walpole, "quite a Roman Palace and
at boundless expense". But he could not refrain from the
caustic remark that it might have been justified as a glorious
apparition at the end of a great and glorious war. As it was,
it was "an insult to poverty and degradation". Still for the
Academicians it was an achievement. And Angelica had
sent six pictures: two classical groups, "Modesty embracing virtuous Love" and two more, "Sybil" and "A Vestal".
She also exhibited a portrait of a lady and her daughter
which cannot now be traced, as well as a design for a fan.
The fan is particularly interesting, for Fanny Burney in her
Journals alludes to it. Sir Joshua had taken "little Burney",
as she was called, to see an exhibition of fans made by
Poggi, the then very fashionable dealer, and she writes, "I
passed the whole day at Sir Joshua Reynolds's with Miss
Palmer, who in the morning took me to see some most
beautiful fans painted by Poggi from designs by Sir Joshua,
Angelica, West, and Cipriani, on leather, they are more
delightful than can well be imagined, one was bespoke by
the Duchess of Devonshire for a present for some woman of
rank in France. It was to cost £30."

13

It was in this year too that Angelica made the acquaintance
of George Keate, probably at the Nollekens, whose great
friend he was. He was a writer who had spent a considerable part of his life abroad; his interests were various for he
was also a naturalist, an antiquary and a poet of sorts. He
was immensely taken with Angelica and published a fulsome poem addressed to her in 1781, which was partially
inspired by a conversation he had with her on the subject of
her colouring. He had accidentally learnt from her that one
of her colours was prepared from the gums which envelop
the mummies brought from Egypt:

> ". . . 'Your Art for ages shall insure
> What Pyramids could not secure,
> The scattered reliques they inshrined
> To your enlivening touch consigned,
>
> Shall in far happier forms appear
> And new existence seem to wear
> From your repute and power derive
> And Egypt's Kings once more revive."

During the last few years Angelica had been making
some new arrangements in her housekeeping, principally in
connection with a young protégée whom she had induced to
come to London to try her fortune. Years before, when she
had been in Florence, she had made the acquaintance of a
Mrs. Hadfield, who had a thriving pensione there. This lady
had a small daughter to whom Angelica was attached, and
whose course she had followed since the child was gifted in
much the same way as that in which she, Angelica, had
been. In the schoolroom she had taken medals for drawing
and in a few years she had become a member of the

Florentine Academy of Fine Arts, and her next step had
been Rome, where she knew James Northcote, who wrote
to Reynolds in 1778. "We have now in Rome a Miss
Hadfield who studies painting. She plays very fairly on the
Harpsichord, and sings and composes music very finely,
and will be another Angelica." Everything was going well
for the young girl when suddenly her father lost all his
money and the family was plunged into ruin. Her career
seemed over, and she even contemplated going into a
cloister.

Angelica, who had always maintained her friendship with
the Hadfields, opposed this step strenuously, and followed
her protests up with an offer of help. She invited the family
to London, and promised to introduce Maria to influential
friends and patrons. She sent money for the journey and
when they arrived settled them in lodgings, and proceeded
to make good her promises. Fortunately her task was not
difficult. Maria was indeed as talented and as pretty as she
had been described; it was not long before she found
commissions and was accepted in artistic circles. It was
during a visit to the house of a remarkable collector,
Charles Townley, that Maria met the man she was to
marry, Richard Cosway. Zoffany has depicted the famous
collector, Charles Townley, seated in his library, surrounded by his treasures, indeed such a forest of antique
statues, marble heads and busts of every sort and shape as
only a palace in Rome could have rivalled. Some of these
can be seen in the British Museum today. But in its
owner's day it was part of an hospitable home, for it was
Townley's custom to gather round his Sunday dinner table
the artists and writers who found their way to 7 Park
Street.[1] If it was really here that Maria and Cosway met,
they lost very little time in courting and were married in
1781 with Angelica there to enjoy the happiness of the girl
she had so generously sponsored.

In 1775 there had been another wedding, for Rosa
Florini, the cousin whom Joseph Johann Kauffmann had
brought with him as an aid to his daughter, was married to

[1] Now Queen Anne's Gate.

another artist, this time an Italian long settled in London, Joseph Bonomi, the architect and Associate of the Academy. This couple had six children and Angelica was godmother to two of them. It was through the Bonomis that Angelica met the future revolutionary, Marat, now living in London as a medico and later veterinary surgeon to the Comte d'Artois, brother of Louis XVI. He had studied medicine in Bordeaux, come to England, taken a rather dubious degree as physician in the University of St. Andrews, and found his way back to London to set up a practice although his degree did not really permit of this.

The eighteenth century in England was a century of gossip, and only a nonentity could hope to avoid it. We have seen the damaging and absurd suggestion that Reynolds and others plotted to trick Angelica into a bogus marriage in order to humble her. An even stranger story confronts us now which can at least be traced to the man who retailed it. It concerns Marat, the blood-stained villain of the September massacres during the French Revolution. He was quite as great a scoundrel as Brandt, but with a political and journalistic ability which were to make him seem a prophet and saviour to many people for a long time, and he maintained that he had seduced Angelica. This is recorded by his friend and fellow republican Jean Pierre Brissot de Warville.

Brissot, famous not only for the part he played in the Revolution as a journalist of the first order, in his memoirs gives us a picture not only of his own complicated life but of the many people he met and knew. From his earliest youth he had hated kings, having read at the age of nine a life of Oliver Cromwell. After graduating from the College of Chartres, he met two Englishmen, who so impressed him that he began the study of the English language and history. He speedily became so proficient that when later he was forced to flee from France, he could easily find a place and friends in London. Here he met another emigré, the equally dedicated republican, Jean Paul Marat.

Brissot writes, "The pride of character of this man, subsequently so famous, made me seek his acquaintance,

Lady Elizabeth Foster. Courtesy of the National Trust, Ickworth.

and we became close friends. Marat recounted to me many of the circumstances of his life, which augmented my esteem for him, and he protested a fervent love of liberty. He had in 1775 published a book which he called *The Chains of Slavery* and in which he denounced the corruption of the Court and Ministry. This work made a great sensation, he said, and had been followed by presentations from towns and Corporations in England, and admission to their ranks. He also spoke to me about his prodigious success in medicine, and said that in Paris he had been paid as much as thirty-five francs for a visit. He spoke to me too about the celebrated Kauffmann, praising not only her talent for music but also for painting, and I have kept these anecdotes."

Unfortunately for us he did not print them in his memoirs, except the outrageous claim made by Marat to have seduced Angelica, who at that time was the fiancée of Marat's friend Antonio Zucchi. To be a painter or a writer in these years was to be particularly fortunate; there was a great deal of money about and the arts were fashionable. The company that gathered at one of their favourite meeting places was easy and hospitable; this was the Old Slaughterhouse Coffee House at the top of St. Martin's Lane. It was chosen for its central position and availability, for the lane had been cleared of its brook when the great Church of St. Martin had been built in 1720, and the lane now housed not a few literati and painters. It was near the palace of Whitehall, and not too far from Somerset House where the exhibitions of the Academy were held, while also nearby the brothers Adam were building on the land they had acquired, afterwards to be called the Adelphi.

The diarist Farington, talking eighteen years afterwards to Hamilton, tells us that here came the Italian Antonio Zucchi and his friend, the architect Bonomi, and very probably we may add, here was sometimes old Joseph Johann Kauffmann, the friend of both. And here a knife and fork were always laid at Zucchi's table for the Frenchman, Marat. He seems to have been particularly friendly with Zucchi, who was perhaps the one of the

7—AK • •

convivial party most likely to understand him. Also Antonio was well off, for he was engaged at this time on the plans for the decoration of the magnificent house Adam was building for Elizabeth, Countess of Home, in Portman Square. So well off indeed that he could be persuaded by the impecunious Marat to lend him money—up to £500 said Hamilton, never repaid, except by scurrilous innuendo against the woman Zucchi was in love with!

Jean Paul spoke very little about his extremely ambiguous career during the ten years he spent in Great Britain. The biographer of his years in England, S. L. Phipson, is at pains to trace his activities and connects him with the Mara or le Maitre who tutored during two years at the flourishing Academy of Warrington. He next is suspected of being the Maitre who stole gold medals from the Ashmolean Museum at Oxford, and was sent for two years' imprisonment in the Thames Hulks. In Scotland he cajoled the rector of St. Andrews' University to grant him a Doctorate of Medicine, on the strength of a pamphlet on "Gleets" in the north. There is a rumour that he was in Harrogate, and here he might first have met Zucchi who was engaged on work at Nostell Priory, at a time when Angelica was decorating Harewood House. In 1776 he published another pamphlet, *A singular Disease of the Eye Produced by Mercurial Preparations*, and appeared in London, calling himself Dr. Marat of Church Street, Soho. He was inordinately proud of his scientific achievements, and with his brilliant conversation and fertile imagination, it is not surprising that he impressed his hearers at the Coffee House.

At this time he produced yet another pamphlet, *Découvertes de M. Marat sur le Feu l'Electricité et la Lumière*, of which he presented a copy inscribed to Angelica, an extraordinarily interesting survival which is reproduced here for the first time. Hamilton told Farington that Marat was often taken by Zucchi to call on her at Golden Square. But it is difficult to imagine that she could have been attracted to this sallow man, pockmarked, with lank black hair and a twitching mouth, though he must have admired her beauty or he would not have been at pains to make his scandalous assertion. A contemptible lie of this pattern came easily enough from the atrocious advocate of the Terror and when Charlotte Corday plunged her knife into his heart she avenged not only the many unfortunates whom he had helped to send to the Guillotine but also this woman who had not a drop of aristocratic blood in her veins and who had done nothing to arouse his hatred and envy. Apart from Brissot's second-hand testimony, there is not a shred of evidence to support the malicious contention. Let this friend have the last word: "I have always been credulous and it is only in reconsidering the diverse circumstances of my acquaintance with this odious man, and on equating them with the role which he played in the Revolution that I have become convinced of the charlatanism which all his life directed his actions and his writings." In throwing this doubt on Marat's credentials and in failing to reveal the anecdotes which the man told him, Brissot strengthens our conviction that the boast of having seduced Angelica was made in a moment of spite, or of fury at her lack of response to his overtures.

14

Angelica by now had both fame, comfort and money. The artist had earned a considerable fortune during her stay in England. It has been assessed at £14,000, no small sum in those days. But she had also her old and ailing father to consider, threatened annually by the English winter. And, as she had said long ago, Rome was ever in her heart. It is likely that at the beginning of 1780 ideas of change were already taking form in her mind, for to the Exhibition of that year she sent only three pictures, one the portrait of a lady as a Muse which Walpole says was the celebrated singer Miss Harrop, and two classical subjects, "Venus attended by the Graces" and "The Judgment of Paris". The reason may have been that she was not really fit to undertake many large canvases; her health was not good and so she was concentrating and very busy on designs for the many engravers; for fans, as we have seen; and for head and tail pieces for chapters in books. A set of engravings entitled "Morning Amusements" belong to this period, and engravings for Boydell's Shakespeare Gallery. In general she seemed dispirited and melancholy, and events which were taking place around her were not much help. It was the moment of the Gordon riots, with Lord George Gordon setting all the west end of London in a turmoil with his marches on the Parliament to protest against the Catholic Relief Bill. The rioting must have terrified her and as a Catholic she had every reason to deprecate it. The dreadful scenes continued throughout the day and the evening brought the fear of general fire. Fortunately the havoc did not go so far, but—and this is where it touches Angelica— the mob forced the Sardinian Chapel in Lincoln's Inn Fields, and gutted it; everything was thrown into the street as food for bonfires; the silver lamps, the benches and books were fuel for the fires inside. They then moved on until they came to Golden Square, where Count Haslang, the Minister from the Elector of Bavaria, had a house and Chapel. This they burnt to the ground, and in plundering his house, found quantities of rum and tea, all contraband, for the old rascal, who had been Minister for forty years, had run a profitable business in smuggling. For Angelica and her father it must have been highly terrifying, as all demented mobs are, and they must have felt the general weakening of law and order and government which had set in as the aftermath of the lamentable American war. The rioting went on for days until on 8 June, when London and Southwark were on fire in six places, the regular troops managed to restore some sort of order—a camp of ten thousand was quartered in Hyde Park—and by the 9th the worst seemed over.

Finally the worry of her father's increasing illness persuaded Angelica that the time for a move had come. With Rosa Fiorini married, the whole care of the household fell on her. Long were the discussions as to the how and when they should make the move. And presently another factor entered their plans. Antonio Zucchi, her collaborator in a great deal of her decorative work, had always been very highly esteemed by old Joseph Johann. He was a Venetian, and his surviving work proves him to have been an artist of no small merit. Her biographer, Rossi says, "He (had) never aspired to Angelica's hand, but was very much in her society." It may be that it was to old Kauffmann that the idea first occurred of a nearer association. Zucchi was not young—he was fifty-five—but then neither was Angelica although she was fifteen years his junior. He was steady and would be a safe guide and friend when her father was gone. From every point of view the match seemed admirable. Did it seem so to Angelica? As she turned it over in her mind, it must have seemed to her like the abandonment of all her youthful hopes. It was a definite step into middle age, a step away from the desires and follies of those days when people had thought her flirtatious, a goodbye, in fact, to love.

By the autumn of 1780 the decision had been made.

They would leave England. It may even have been that this country which had done so much for her reputation had become distasteful to her. She would keep her best English friends and patrons but there must have been much which she was only too anxious to forget. But the serious illness of her father postponed Angelica's arrangements, and 30 October finds her writing to a close friend, Mrs. Fordyce, that after all the hurry and preparation for her journey, she was still there; her comfort was that she was still among her friends. The postscript to her letter reads, "The Fatal Moment of parting is not so near as I thought it would have been. So that before months or years do pass I may have the happiness of seeing you."

In fact the winter saw Angelica hard at work as usual. Antonio had proposed and been accepted, but neither of the parties seemed eager to marry, and indeed the marriage appears to be more of a part of the general plan than any urgent wish on her suitor's part. Zucchi wrote to his Patron, Sir Rowland Winn, saying how agreeable Angelica was to him, and how happy the union would make him, and equally how highly he esteemed her as an artist. If there was nothing that could be called ardent love, there was certainly already true affection.

On 10 July 1781 the die was cast. She married Zucchi. She had opted for safety and wisdom. The Indenture Tripartite sets forth the marriage settlement between Antonio Zucchi of St. Ann's parish, Soho, painter, and Angelica Kauffmann, of Golden Square, Bloomsbury, painter, on the other hand, with the signatures of her trustees. They were George Keate Esq., Peter Kuliff, merchant, and Daniel Braithwaite, of the General Post Office, and it was agreed:

> "To put in their hands as trustees the sum of £3350 three per cent consolidated annuities, as well as £1650 three per cent consolidated bank annuities—
> For the use and benefit of said Angelica Kauffmann whether sole or covert. And to enable her to enjoy the dividends thereof exclusive of the said Antonio Zucchi,

her intended husband, who is not to intermeddle therewith, nor any part thereof to be subject to his debts; and is also to give her power to leave the said sums by will as she shall appoint."

The document is signed and sealed by

> Antonio Zucchi
> Angelica Kauffmann
> George Keate
> Henry Peter Kuliff
> D. Braithwaite.

All this shows that Angelica had a provident father and a good lawyer, whatever Zucchi may have thought of the actual wording.

He on his part possessed considerable assets—a freehold house in John Street, Adelphi, which was let for £90 a year, also some annuities which brought in £150 a year. Thus both the contracting parties were very comfortably off. Angelica had saved £5,000, and Zucchi about £8,000. They had lived comfortably, and could look forward to renewed and profitable activity in Italy, in which country they were eventually to settle. Their immediate goal was Schwarzenberg, for Kauffmann had a longing to see his old home and friends once more; then they planned to travel to Venice and from there to Rome and Naples.

The *Morning Herald* announced that the marriage had taken place, and in the true spirit of journalism planted a quiver in the minds of the public and the departing group. "She has long refused many advantageous offers of various suitors," it said, "and among them one from Sir Joshua Reynolds who at the same time that he admired her style of painting thought Angelica a divine subject to adorn the hymeneal temple." None of the three people most concerned replied to this boutade and the whole question remains open to conjecture to this day.

15

She would not see London again. Her more severe critics would say that her facile success there had been very largely due to her personal charm, her lively participation in social life and the admiration of a few important figures in the artistic world of London. She had been the "rage". But she herself can never have imagined that this was sufficient foundation on which to build a lifetime's success. Such a public is fickle. Indeed she had already been supplanted in this shallow society, and Maria Cosway was the reigning beauty and toast in the artistic world. As a mature individual, Angelica could evaluate luxury, snobbism, friendship, true and false, real and superficial learning. She knew the type of man who followed his talent with a deep sense of its real importance; and the type who valued it solely for the worldly success and money it could bring. In a word, she was not to be deceived. It has been suggested that by now she was a "sad-eyed, careworn woman". This is almost certainly untrue. Now and always she lived for her work, and of that she had plenty. As an artist she was still in great demand, and she took with her on her journey various half-finished orders, which were to set the new clients crowding to her door.

The packing was done, the last tearful goodbyes were said, the last farewell parties attended, and the group set off, first for Schwarzenberg, where old Joseph Johann persuaded himself that she would spend happy days with his relatives and friends. They braved the uncomfortable crossing to Ostend and stayed a while in the Flanders towns so that Angelica might see the masterpieces they contained. Then on to Thionville where they had relatives, and still on through Germany, across the border into Switzerland, until at last they were in the Grisons and at home once more.

Angelica hesitating between the arts of music and painting. Courtesy of Lord St. Oswald, Nostell Priory.

Schwartzenberg was not changed outwardly, although the narrow path they had trod the first time had now become a road. But alas, old Kauffmann found the fate which awaits many a returning exile. The old friends he had longed to see were many of them no longer there, and not even the new young faces could replace them. Equally, for his daughter there were few attractions; she was not a lover of the countryside, and sitters there were none. So after a short stay the party set off once more towards the South, their real objective. They travelled through the Bavarian highlands in the lovely autumn weather to Innsbrück where they rested two days, then on over the Alps, a fairly hazardous undertaking, burdened as they were with a sick old man. The inns were full and not clean, though the food in general was good and the innkeepers complaisant. Often they must have arrived to find no rooms and been obliged to pass on to the next village in the hope of better luck. But once Verona was reached, they had the prospect of a calm voyage down the Brenta, passing on their way through peaceful villages and past magnificent houses of Venetian magnates, and arriving at last at their destination, Venice. There they were met by Zucchi's relatives, people of a certain affluence and enjoying a high reputation in the city.

Angelica's relief at being at last able to settle down, to get out her easel and commence work on the canvases she had brought from England, was diminished by the state of her father's health. The poor old man had been so disappointed by his lack of pleasure in Schwarzenberg that it rapidly worsened and even the arrival of his sister, Madame Bonomi's mother, did nothing to cheer him. She and his devoted daughter nursed him, but it was of no avail, and in January 1782 he passed away, to his daughter's despair. So long they had been together, so deep had been his love that she felt as if the earth had opened under her feet; her main support had gone. Matters were made worse by the death very shortly after of her aunt, who, old and weakened by her brother's death and the fatigues of nursing him, died barely a month after.

Like most artists she sought relief from her worries in

work and indeed she had hardly settled in Venice than
clients crowded in upon her; her fame had preceded her.
Among the first callers in her studio were the Grand Duke
and Duchess Paul of Russia, travelling in Europe under the
name of the Comte and Comtesse du Nord. The Grand
Duchess fell in love with Angelica, a tribute to the charm
and intelligence which she seemed to radiate, and nothing
would satisfy her and the Grand Duke but that the picture
which she was just then finishing should be theirs. It was
"Leonardo da Vinci expiring in the arms of Francis I", the
sketch for which she had shown at the Royal Academy. But
this work had already been commissioned by another patron
and Angelica could only promise that a further copy should
be painted and sent to St. Petersburg. Then the Grand
Duchess insisted that she must have her portrait by the
beloved artist for, said she, it would serve as a reminder of
one so rare and delightful. This also Angelica was forced to
refuse: she was overwhelmed with orders, but promised to
deliver the work when they were both in Rome.

We have a list which Angelica left behind her of all the
pictures which she painted after her departure from
England. The Grand Duke not only acquired the commissioned Da Vinci for which he paid 460 Venetian zecchini,
but he ordered two others, both scenes from English history, "Queen Eleanor on the point of death from the poison
she had sucked from the wounded Edward I", and the
"Queen recovered from the poison with the help of an
antidote, brought to the King who was in mortal grief
believing that she had passed away".

In Venice too, Angelica made the acquaintance of one of
her most serious patrons, Mr. Bowles of the Grove,
Wanstead, whose enthusiasm for her work became so great
that at one time he seemed to own almost all her best
pictures. He was wealthy, a connoisseur of works of art and
an impassioned collector. His collection eventually fell into
the hands of Sir Charles Cockerell who, after the death of
the third Lord Northwick, assumed the name of Rushout.
Almost all the pictures then came into the market. Miss
Gerard, at the end of the last century, traced a few of them,

but Manners and Williamson, writing in 1924 state that most of the fifty he possessed could not then be traced.

Busy as she might be in Venice, and well received in its most important families, she had no intention of making any prolonged stay. And so in 1782 she and her husband set their faces southwards towards Rome. They stayed in the city for a short time, long enough to find a house near the Spanish Steps, and to attend to its decorating and furnishing. Angelica possessed valuable pictures and beautiful furniture and she had moreover the money left to her by her father, some three thousand five hundred pounds, so she was able to make her prospective home both elegant and comfortable, and not to stint on decoration, in which she was a past mistress. It would have been inconceivable that she, who had helped in the decorating of some of the finest houses in England, could have been satisfied with anything poor or mean. They then left for Naples.

On arriving in Naples she found that, just as in Venice, her reputation had preceded her. Hardly was she there than she received a message from the Queen. Maria Caroline, daughter of the Empress Maria Theresa and sister of the Queen of France, Marie Antoinette, was herself an accomplished amateur, and possessed a large collection of engravings from Angelica's paintings; so Her Majesty lost no time in endeavouring to persuade Angelica to accept an official position at Court—the last thing the painter would be likely to concede. Such an invitation is more evidence of the extremely high esteem in which Angelica was held wherever she went, and the fact that she could refuse such an honour shows too that she was now so well off that she had no need to take anything less than an independent position. Her biographer, Rossi, says that at this time she was "a woman still in the prime of life but without brilliancy of colouring and with a grave and pensive expression". This would not be unusual in a loving person who had recently suffered a double bereavement. But that it is a description of Angelica for the rest of her life is most unlikely. The best part of her days was coming. Her reception in Rome was to be a triumph. Six years later, in

1788, she painted the portrait of herself which now hangs in the Uffizi Gallery in Florence, and which shows us the artist seated on a stone in a landscape, in one hand a portfolio with sketches, in the other a pencil. Rossi comments, "The face is sad and weary, full of resignation almost approaching despair, the pleasing gaiety and attractive beauty of her early days gone, washed away by one surging wave of sorrow." But in our opinion there is no such misery, only the picture of a thoughtful woman still with the beauty of her youthful colouring, and with a reflective attitude which a person of forty years of age might well show.

She set up her studio in Naples and we may be sure that she hung in her room the little picture by Leonardo Da Vinci which represented St. Jerome, which she always carried with her and hung where she could see it constantly, though, when she was absent, it was veiled by a silken cloth. Her life was full, for she copied and studied pictures in the Capodimonte Museum, glad to be among her classical subjects again, and remembering no doubt her early enthusiasm for Winckelmann whose tragic end had occurred in 1768. She set to work at once on the splendid commission she had received from the Queen, for that lady was not accustomed to being kept waiting; it was to paint a group of the whole royal family, a tremendous undertaking for the figures in it were to be life size. She began work on it in September and October 1782 and says herself that she first painted them each singly on separate canvases and then grouped them into one large picture which today hangs in the palace of Caserta. It shows the King, just returned from the hunt; the Queen, seated and surrounded by her children. Princess Maria Theresa, named after her illustrious grandmother, is playing the harp; her sister, Princess Louisa, holds the infant Princess Amalia in her arms; the Prince Royal, Don Francisco, stands by his father and plays with a greyhound; Donna Christina leans against the Queen's side and little Prince Gennaro sits on a cushion and amuses himself with a canary, tied with a ribbon and to which he is giving partial liberty to fly. It is an extremely fine composition, worthy of Gainsborough or Reynolds, even if it suggests a pleasant English country house scene; and even if the King, whose boorish manners were well known, has not a hair out of place, while the Queen, whose *embonpoint* was already beginning to tell, is as slender and as un-Hapsburg as any English lady.

Her work on the Royal picture was by no means the end of her commitments. Mr. Bowles had commissioned six more ovals of classical themes and another Englishman two more oval pictures with scenes from Shakespeare's plays, one from *Coriolanus* and the other from the *Tempest*. Sir William Hamilton, the Envoy Extraordinary of His Britannic Majesty at Naples, also commissioned a picture from her.

Hamilton, a notable figure in Neapolitan society, was a man of extreme erudition and taste: his house was a treasure house of antiquities, and to him belonged at this time the honour of possessing the famous Portland Vase, today in the British Museum. Now he commissioned a picture from Angelica, "Penelope at work assisted by two of her maidens", and the artist must have felt flattered to be included in the collection of such a connoisseur, for she would not take a fee for it. Her picture obviously pleased Sir William and he probably wrote to his friend, William Beckford of Fonthill, about it. In a letter from Beckford, the eccentric author of Vathek says, "as for Angelica, she is my Idol; so say everything that can be said in my name and tell her how I long to see Telemachus's Papa, and all the noble family". It is not certain what he meant, since no picture of Ulysses came from her brush at the time; but perhaps the theme of Hamilton's picture led Beckford to hope for one.

During Angelica's first period in Rome, she had been young enough to be greatly influenced by the important painters working there, like Batoni. From the moment of her return to that city her work had begun to show new strength: without losing her spontaneity and freshness, perhaps partly because she was happy but also because she was older, more experienced, and was a little less the

"Paintress of the Soul" and more of a highly conscious professional. It shows in her later pictures as for example in the Holstein Beck group. This was the largest picture Angelica ever attempted after the Neapolitan Royal Family. It was painted for the Princess of Holstein Beck, a devoted admirer. This lady, a figure of imposing presence and overweening pride, was cousin of the Czar, daughter of the reigning Prince of Holstein and wife of Ivan Bariatinsky. Her two children both figure in the picture. The whole composition is expressive of Angelica's "new style", the classical drapery of the curtains, the marble bust of the Princess's father, the clarity of the grouping and colouring. Angelica took enormous trouble over this picture, and well she might, for the Princess was a terrifying, imperious lady, of whom it was told that when her death was announced to her bailiff he died of joy on the spot.[1]

[1] The picture attained a posthumous fame when it was cited in a book by a German writer, Edouard Engels, who described it as Angelica Kauffmann and the circle of her friends at Castel Gondolfo. The seated figure he asserted was the painter herself whilst a standing lady was Maddalena Riggi, and the two gentlemen her brother and the Councillor Reiffenstein. The mistake was repeated in various journals and even exhibitions, until it was finally laid to rest by Andrea Busiri Vici, of Rome, in an article published in English in the Apollo Magazine March 1963. A sketch for the picture is in the Vorarlberger Museum in Bregenz and the picture itself in Lausanne. Rossi noted that R. Morghen did an elegant engraving of it.

16

The big picture for the Royal Family was not completed when Angelica and Zucchi left Naples. In December 1782 she was back in her own house, and pleased to be settled with all her favourite belongings around her, where she could receive visitors in a worthy way. They were quick to come and of the most distinguished sort. The Emperor of Austria then visiting the city and doubtless advised by his sister, Queen Maria Caroline, lost no time in paying her a visit. When he learned that she had been born in the Grisons, at the time under Austrian control, he claimed her as a subject, and commissioned, in the most flattering terms, two pictures for his gallery in Vienna, leaving the choice of subjects to her, only stipulating that they should be finished quickly. To this she was forced to reply that she could not promise them at once, since she had the Neapolitan picture in hand and also a commission for the Empress Catherine of Russia, both of which must be completed first. The Emperor was forced to accept this excuse and only received his pictures two years later.

The Rome to which she and Zucchi returned was not much different from that which she had left twenty years before except that it had slid a little further towards decadence. The new ideas which were permeating Europe since the publication of Rousseau's *Contrat Social* in 1767 had reached even the Papal States, and though successive Popes had tried to stem the rising tide of criticism, their efforts had resulted in little more than protest. The enmity of the Protestant powers of Europe and even of some of the Catholic powers was directed mainly against the Jesuits, whose work knew no frontiers and whose fine schools and teaching threatened the "philosophers" and free thinkers. The monastic orders too were against them. The war against the Jesuits was a long one, too long to enter into here. It is enough to say that in 1773 the Pope Clement XIV yielded to pressure put upon him as much from the Catholic powers of France, Spain, Naples and Parma as from certain Protestant states, and dissolved the Order. The forces of liberalism had won. His grief helped to kill the Pontiff and a new Pope was elected, Cardinal Braschi, who became Pius VI. He was a very different man from his predecessor. Handsome and worldly, he aimed at being loved and admired, at patronising the arts, at being a second Julius II. He married one of his nephews to a brilliant wife and for them built a magnificent palace, the Palazzo Braschi, he adorned St. Peter's and laid out the gardens of the Vatican and he beautified the squares of Rome and built the steps of the Trinità dei Monti. His crowning achievement was the draining of the Pontine Marshes, that home of malaria, and he used the ground thus gained to encourage the foundation of workshops and all sorts of industry, thus adding to the prosperity of the city. The population increased, as did also the possibility of a better life; though the dirt and pauperism still existed, they were familiar evils, hardly noticed except by visitors. The visitors too increased, led by more crowned heads than ever before. The Emperor was followed by the Czar, the King of Sweden, and the sons of the King of England, and they were emulated by half the aristocracy of Europe. The Eternal City welcomed them all—and profited from them. And the artists had a heyday. Only the Church felt the mutterings of doom and listened to the bad news from France.

In her salon, Angelica entertained with conversation and music the cream of Roman and artistic society, and any visiting celebrity was taken there as a matter of course. There is less evidence that she and her husband participated to any extent in the life of the hordes of artists who then lived—or existed—in Rome. They forgathered in the clubs and cafés, each nationality choosing its favourite meeting place, and settling mostly around the Piazza di Spagna where also the artistically-minded visitors and patrons

The Marchioness Townshend and her eldest son, Lord William Townshend as Cupid. The child only sat for the face, as his mother was frightened he would catch cold. The body is that of another boy, a Master Clarke, obtained for the purpose. Courtesy of the Marquess of Exeter.

Benjamin West. Courtesy of the National
rait Gallery, London.

25. Batoni's portrait of the 1st Earl of Charlemont.
Courtesy of Ralph Cabrera Jr., New York.

The 4th Earl of Bristol, Bishop of Cloyne and
ry. Courtesy of the National Trust, Ickworth

27. Dr. August Tissot. Courtesy of the Musée
Cantonal des Beaux-Arts, Lausanne.

28. King Ferdinand IV of Naples and Sicily and his family. Courtesy of the Prince of Liechtenstein, Vadu

29. Head of an Apostle, in the parish church of Schwarzenberg.

30. The Penitent Magdalen. Author's collectio

31. Ceiling at Rathfarnham Castle, Dublin. Courtesy of the Society of Jesus.

32. *Below left*. Vienna Chocolate cup and cover with saucer painted by Joseph Leithner after works attributed to Angelica. Date: 1804. Courtesy of The Antique Company of New York, Inc.

33. *Below right*. Flower vase. Courtesy of the Victoria and Albert Museum.

34. Portrait of a Lady as Hebe. Author's collection.

35. Cupid Bound. Courtesy of Professor and Mrs. T. Gilmartin, Dublin.

36. *Above*. Margaret, Countess of Lucan. By permission of the Earl Spencer.
37. *Right*. Mary, 3rd Duchess of Richmond. From Goodwood House, by courtesy of the Trustees.

38. "Painting". In the ceiling of the Central Hall of the Royal Academy. This and "Design" are reproduced by courtesy of the Royal Academy of Arts, London.

39. "Design". In the ceiling of the Central Hall of the Royal Academy.

40. *Above*. Venus appearing to Aeneas on the road to Carthage. Courtesy of the Vorarlberger Handel·
kammer, Feldkirch.

41. *Top right*. The Parting of Hector and Andromache. Courtesy of the Saltram Collection, Nation·
Trust, Plymouth.

42. *Bottom right*. Telemachus crowned by the Nymphs of Calypso. Courtesy of the Metropolitan Museu·
of Art, New York. Bequest of Collis P. Huntington.

43. Cleopatra before Augustus. Courtesy of the University of Kansas Museum of Art.

4. The parting of Abelard and Eloise. At the Hermitage, Leningrad. Courtesy of the Novosti Press
gency.

45. *Above*. Design for a fan. Courtesy of Christie, Manson & Woods.
46. *Below*. Fan painted by Angelica. Courtesy of Christie, Manson & Woods.

47. *Top right*. Table painted by Angelica. Courtesy of the Countess Waldegrave, Chewton House, Chewton Mendip.
48. *Bottom right*. Painting by Angelica on a Broadwood Piano. Courtesy of the Metropolitan Museum of Art, New York. Gift of Curtis Freshel.

Porcelain figure of two nymphs adorned the
~~~e of Pan. After one of Angelica's pictures.
~~rtesy of the Victoria and Albert Museum,
~~don.

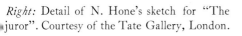

Right: Detail of N. Hone's sketch for "The
~~juror". Courtesy of the Tate Gallery, London.

~~osite page

   Top: The Dying Gaul. Courtesy of the
~~itoline Museum, Rome
   Left: The Appollo Belvedere. Courtesy of the
~~ican.
   Far left: The Portland Vase in the British
~~seum. Courtesy of the Trustees. All were
~~ences on Angelica.

54. Design for Goethe's "Egmont". Courtesy of
Mrs. Hladick Hämmerle.

55. Engraving of an old man. Courtesy of Shane Flynn.

56. Wedgwood plaque showing a typical neo-classical design.

57. Part of a Meissen tea set with reproductions of "Cupid Bound". Courtesy of Peter Bander. These show the tremendous influence that Angelica was having and continued to have in Europe throughout the 19th century.

58. Engraving of the portrait of the Hon. Anne Damer. Engraved by T. Ryder.

9. Sketch for the
ortrait of the Hon.
nne Damer. Author's
ollection.

10. Copy of Marat's "Découvertes" inscribed by him to
ngelica. Courtesy of Dr. Federico Zeri.

DÉCOUVERTES
DE M. MARAT,
*Docteur en Médecine & Médecin des Gardes-
du-Corps de MONSEIGNEUR LE
COMTE D'ARTOIS.*
SUR LE FEU,
L'ÉLECTRICITÉ ET LA LUMIÈRE,
Constatées par une suite
D'EXPÉRIENCES NOUVELLES
*Qui viennent d'être vérifiées par MM. les Commissaires
de l'Académie des Sciences.*

A PARIS,
DE L'IMPRIMERIE DE CLOUSIER,
RUE SAINT-JACQUES.
M. DCC. LXXIX.

61. Tischbein's drawing of Goethe's studio in Rome. Courtesy of the Goethe Nationalmuseum, Weima

62. The Ballroom at Abbeyville, with two oval paintings by Angelica. Courtesy of Mr. Charles Haughe
Photo: Clair Studios, Dublin.

63. Lady Betty Cobbe. Courtesy of Mrs. Joan Cobbe, Newbridge House.

Much Respected Friend.

August the 13

It is a long time I wished to thank you in a private letter for all the Kindness and care you take concerning my little affairs in England. I am happy to know that you are well, I wish you joy to your new acquisition at Highgate the situation is beautiful. may you enjoy it in health and contentment with those who are dear to you. as for the few points of mine the which you have destined to adorn your Drawing Room. the may perhaps serve to keep me in your remembrance. how glad should I be to pay you and Mr. Hussavison at Highgate. — I shall however with my thoughts be often with ye.. and rejoice our happiness. have you no thoughts to visite Italy —? I confess I should be glad we could all meet once more before we depart from this globe - all is possible in the mean time I beg the continuance of your friendship. present my kindest compt. to my worthy friend Mr. Hussaff. and to your Son. with every sentiment of gratitud. I am . sir for ever your very obliged serv. Angelica Kauffman

64. A letter from Angelica Kauffmann. Courtesy of the Hyde Collection, Four Oaks Farm, New Jersey

found lodgings. Then as now they congregated on the steps where they chattered like starlings, or in the Café Inglese which had been patronised by Winckelmann and Mengs, and where Hamilton and Jenkins met to discuss their gains or losses in the lucrative trade in antiques which the former engaged in. The Zucchis aspired to a rather more selective society; to their house came distinguished visitors, and possibly also the younger and not so well-known, because revolutionary, artists of the time. Such were Canova and David, and some of the English like Flaxman. Angelica was made a member of the strange society in Rome called the "Arcadians" presided over by the Abbé Godard. So too was Goethe when he arrived and we have this account of his reception into it and the diploma which he received showing his membership. When he arrived in Rome, he tells us, "the society had existed for exactly a century. It had often changed its places of meeting and its artistic ideals, but it still maintained its outward form with great respectability if not with equal prestige. There were few distinguished foreign residents in Rome who had not been inveigled into joining it." Goethe became an Arcadian Shepherd in 1786, observing that it was the contributions of their foreign members "which provided the custodian of these poetic acres with a modest income". Madame de Stael, when she came to the city, was invited to one of its gatherings and asked to recite something, but Vernon Lee in her *Studies of the Eighteenth Century in Italy* takes a poor view of the later days of the society, telling us, "The Arcadians all met at the Bosco Paradisio. Heterogeneous, cosmopolitan and rather frivolous Arcadians, very unlike those Metastasio had seen there sixty years before; English milordi led about by tutors, German princes led about by equerries, artists, antiquaries of all nations, Angelica Kauffmann, Piranesi, Gavin Hamilton, Tischbein, Zeoga, the Danish archaeologist, and a motley crowd, not knowing very well, nor caring very much, what this Arcadian business might be."

Angelica had returned to Rome at a time of extraordinary energy in the art world; great houses were being enlarged and the new rooms needed decoration. This was

8—AK * *

mainly supplied by the Romans, who kept this field very much their province, and though Angelica had excelled in such work while in England she had no such commissions now. She was in any case kept much too busy. In February 1783, she painted the celebrated Dr. Tissot of Lausanne, a man much esteemed by Voltaire; then came two more pictures for members of the Gaetani family and a large picture for the Prime Minister of Naples, and other members of the Neapolitan nobility, among them the Queen's Mistress of the Robes, who asked for a portrait of the little Infante Don Giuseppe who had recently died. Commissions came now in twos and threes; Count Potocki of Poland requested a portrait of his daughter standing by a monument recently erected to his dead wife. Then came two for an Italian, Count Chiesi; and three English travellers, Sir James Graham, a young Englishman making the Grand Tour, his tutor, the Reverend Thomas Brand; and another sitter to whom she refers as "an English nobleman".

However busy Angelica was, it is impossible to imagine that she could have completely avoided seeing the festivities of the Roman Carnival, so celebrated in song and story. The streets were everywhere full of the populace, masked and disguised, the aristocrats in their coaches throwing confetti and sugar plums at the intoxicated crowds on the sidewalks. The Carnival was authorised by the Church and recognised by the State. It was ushered in by Senators and the Governor of Rome, and the procession along the Corso, richly decorated with tapestries and flowers, gave promise of orgies to come. Everyone except Jews, prostitutes and Churchmen might wear disguise, and the variety of these travesties was surprising, men dressed up as women and women as men. Rank was forgotten, women paraded with little switches made of rushes with which they tickled the noses of the men and, as Madame de Stael remarked, all were confounded together, turning the nation upside down as if there were no social order any more. But the fun was good-natured and it went on until the highlight of all, the races to be run by Barbery coursers from the obelisk in the Piazza del Popolo to the Piazza Venezia. The horses were riderless, full of oats and even stimulated by drugs, and with fireworks going on along the whole of the course. The crowd, wild, intoxicated with noise, colour, and movement, oblivious to accident from flying hooves or snapping jaws, drove the maddened steeds on till finally at the Piazza they were stopped by cloths stretched across the road and the winner was declared. The owner was presented with the *Palio*, the prize, a golden saddle cloth, and the victorious steed returned to his stable, prancing nobly through the streets. Something approaching this may still be seen in the Palio of Siena today. Suddenly on the stroke of twelve on Shrove Tuesday all was over. Lights were extinguished and on the morrow everyone went piously to church. Even hard-working Angelica must have enjoyed some of this revelry.

The Neapolitan Royal Family were delighted with their group when it was brought to them at last by the Zucchis and it was paid for during the first days of November 1784, with 4,317 Neapolitan ducats and the gift of a most regal jewel with the Queen's initials in diamonds and surrounded by twelve big diamonds beautifully mounted. The value of the jewel, notes Angelica, was estimated at 700 ducats. And this payment, handsome as it was, did not end the Queen's complaisance towards the artist. She wished to keep her always by her, lodged her in the charming Palazzo Francavilla, with its view over the beautiful Bay and wide gardens, and tried by every means in her power to tempt Angelica to remain in Naples. When she was unable to force this she entreated her to stay long enough to give lessons in drawing to the elder princesses, and to this Angelica agreed. Maria Carolina hoped that in this way she had won her point. She frequently sat with her children during the lessons, and she may have profited herself from the instruction. More presents of jewels followed and this went on until it was time for the Court to move to the summer palace of Caserta.

But here Angelica was firm. Rome called her, art called her, and her determination was strengthened by an illness which had gripped her, a fever, brought on possibly by the

miasmas which arose from the horrible sanitary conditions
in the town. In this illness she was attended by a Dr. Cirillo,
a most distinguished man and able physician, one of the
greatest scientific men of the day.

Back in Rome again, in her own house and with her
friends, who had missed her sadly, Angelica's popularity
can be judged by Mrs. Piozzi's comment when visiting the
Eternal City: "I must not quit Rome however without a
word of Angelica Kauffmann . . . Beside her paintings, of
which all the world has been the judge, her conversation
attracts all people of taste to her house which none can bear
to leave without difficulty and regret." She was universally
loved and admired, and her life seemed to have reached a
peak of happiness and stability after so much turmoil and
deception. But there was a certain element of restlessness in
it. She found the air of Rome unhealthy for too long a
period, and her husband bought for her a small property at
Castel Gandolfo, not too far from the city. Then too the
refreshment of picnics at Frascati, or Tivoli, or nearer
Hadrian's Villa, where the artists loved to go on the long
sunny Sundays to escape the town's heat, delighted her.
Still more a visit to the fantastic home of Cardinal Albani,
that treasure house arranged by Winckelmann for his
patron, where the palatial rooms of many coloured rare
marbles contained the unmatched wonders of art through
the centuries. Here were the finest works of Grecian and
Graeco Roman art, statues, heads, masks, bas reliefs. Pictures too—not even the Vatican could show finer. And
surrounding the palace marvellous gardens, their groves
and fountains luring the eye and inviting the visitor to enjoy
their cool shades.

Angelica's life now took on a settled character. She had
her husband to rely on for all the details of the household;
he did all the ordering and certainly cared for her comfort.
But even more than this, she had beside her a man whom
she could trust absolutely and who was fully capable of
advising her not only in details of her life, but in her art.
For Zucchi was a capable painter himself. These two, so
intimately associated not only in their lives but in their art,

formed a fruitful comradeship, he attending to all the practical affairs, such as buying the canvases and frames for her pictures and solving the difficulties of transport, but leaving her free to concentrate on her painting and music and the entertainment of their guests.

Presently it was time to revisit Naples, taking with her two pictures for the Queen, one again the "Mother of the Gracchi," the other of Julia, the wife of Pompey, fainting at the sight of his bloodstained garment. The Queen received her with open arms, gave her the use of the Palazzo Francavilla for the second time. Once again she was urged to remain. Maria Carolina was a woman of strong desires and accustomed to consideration and even subserviency from those who surrounded her. She was the third of the Austrian Arch-Duchesses, Maria Theresa's daughters, to be affianced to the young King Ferdinand of the Two Sicilies. The first two had died one after the other of smallpox, and the Empress who was determined on the Bourbon alliance, was forced to make another choice among her remaining daughters. Ferdinand was not unduly upset by the loss of his earlier brides-to-be; he only revolted against the loss of his hunting during an obligatory day of mourning. He was equally apathetic when a third Arch-Duchess was chosen for him—Maria Carolina, nineteen months younger than himself, and the favourite sister of Maria Antonia—Marie Antoinette. This particular Arch-Duchess had given her mother a considerable amount of trouble. She was intelligent, but wilful and imperious, and had been separated from her younger sister because she incited her to revolt against nursery rules, playing tricks and inventing unsuitable amusements. She set out from Vienna with a heavy heart, her august mother's last advice was "Avoid coquetry; love your husband and be firmly attached to him, that is the only true happiness on earth." But earlier she had admitted: "I regard her as a sacrifice to politics; if she does her duty to God and her husband and ensures the safety of her soul, I will be satisfied, even if she is not happy." The journey was not too unpleasant, and at Florence Caroline was entertained by her brother, the

Grand Duke Leopold. She charmed everyone, including Sir Horace Mann, who wrote to Horace Walpole, "She is a most amiable Queen, but it is feared that her delicacy and good sense will only make her feel the want of both in her Royal Consort, whose deficiency in both has made many people interpret it as an organical defect, approaching madness on some occasions."

And indeed the shock was so terrible on her arrival that in her first letter home she wrote: "I pray that my little Antonia will never have to suffer what I have suffered in the first weeks of my marriage." Her husband was ugly, coarse, and ill-educated, having been governed by a tutor who had indulged his every whim while neglecting his instruction from a fear that he might lose his influence over his pupil. So he had grown up in the company of grooms and servants, loving stupid practical jokes and of course surrounded by sycophantic courtiers.

Maria Carolina took her husband's measure and she proceeded to put her mother's advice into practice. She appeared to sympathise with Ferdinand's childish games, flattered him about his hunting triumphs, and gradually led him to believe that she loved him. From then on it was easy: with the aid of the redoubtable Prime Minister, the Marchese Tanucci, she ruled the country. In 1778 another remarkable man appeared in Naples, this was Captain John Acton, sent from Tuscany by the Grand Duke "in order to give his advice and assistance towards the putting of His Sicilian Majesty's marine on a respectable footing". The Queen was enchanted with him from the first, he was just what she needed, together they would create a new Kingdom. An able and experienced administrator, he was a bachelor and man of the world, and at forty-two, in the prime of life. He was of course credited with being her lover, but since his manner was cool and impenetrable, no one could be certain. There was wild gossip, but in a Court which hummed with rumours, where love affairs were the rule and not the exception, and everybody knew who was sleeping with whom, this was hardly surprising. The Queen was producing a child every year, a state hardly conducive to amorous adventure, and when Angelica came to Naples she found the six charming children that we see in her picture.

Her second stay in Naples was very much a repetition of her first. Once more she was begged to remain, but would not. Despite this second refusal, Angelica seems always to have cherished pleasant memories of the Queen and her generosity. Her Majesty presented her with a magnificent cross in diamonds as a sign of appreciation of the work she had done with the princesses; and she paid her splendidly for the pictures she had ordered. She enjoyed the company to be met in Naples. Here she encountered Count Paul Skavronsky and his wife, the beautiful niece of Prince Potemkin, the all-powerful favourite of the Empress of Russia. She was commissioned to paint the Countess who was accounted the most lovely woman in Europe, and this and her importance, as the wife of the Ambassador to Naples and the relation of so outstanding a personage as her uncle, doubtless influenced Angelica in her decision to devote more than ordinary care to her work. She painted the Countess twice, once alone and then with her little girl of four years old sitting beside her mother and presenting her with a bunch of flowers. Another sitter, almost as beautiful as the Countess, was Lady Elizabeth Foster, afterwards Duchess of Devonshire, for whom she began a half length portrait with the isle of Ischia in the background. This leads us to suppose that the Zucchis may have made a visit to the fabulous island with its extinct volcano either with Lady Elizabeth Foster or alone. In any case, the allusion to the island must have had some personal significance. However, the pull of Rome was too strong, and by November 1785 Angelica was back at her easel and painting away; first a portrait of Princess Gagarin with her baby—she held the child close to her while he played with a hound. The charm and naturalness of these pictures of young women with their children is indescribable, in some way Angelica does not seem to have been disturbed, by the babble of infants in the studio; a gift which is not given to all painters.

The year 1786 showed no slackening of work. In January she finished a portrait of the Prince Poniatowsky of Poland, the nephew of the King, resplendent in his uniform with the medal of St. Stanislas, a model for a full length figure to be delivered later. Russians, Germans, Poles jostle each other in her lists, mostly portraits, but for the Duke de Chaulnes of Paris she painted two pictures, one of Venus and Adonis, when the goddess tries to persuade him not to go hunting during her absence, the other of Circe with Ulysses, who is lying on a couch while food is being prepared after the manner of the ancients.

Not only was Angelica occupied with pressing commissions from daily visitors, but she was at work on the second picture for the Emperor Joseph II of Austria. This was "The return of Arminius after his conquest of the legion of Varro". Its companion would be "The funeral honours paid to Pallas by Aeneas". Whether she chose these subjects because of some connection with a conversation she had had with His Majesty, or whether they just appealed to her, we cannot know. The Emperor was an extraordinary man, liberal, and so ascetic in his tastes that he caused much confusion in the Courts he visited. At Versailles he had demanded a camp bed and a rough covering, with one attendant. Here in Rome, he was the guest of the Pope, and when His Holiness had shown him the treasures of the Vatican they repaired to St. Peter's to pray. The Prelate took the Emperor to a cushioned faldstool and knelt, but his guest threw the cushions away and knelt on the bare floor. "I always use the cushions," remonstrated the Pope. "You can do as you like," replied the Emperor, "I do this." But he was generous to others, and when the pictures had arrived in Vienna and had been hung in the Imperial Gallery they were paid for immediately by Colonel Hartzen, who also brought as a gift a beautiful jewel with his monogram set in diamonds and a handsome gold chain, also a gold snuff box and a letter saying that the pictures had been placed in an important position and were viewed by all with great satisfaction and admiration as being the work of an Austrian woman who had attained the highest position and accomplishment in the art of painting. Angelica's heart swelled with pride and we may be sure that she regretted that her devoted father was not alive to enjoy and to hear such praise. The year ended as it had begun, with more and more portraits being demanded. Her life was indeed full.

But with all this agreeable intercourse her work must continue in the background. In April she painted the Duke of Gloucester's two children. He was the brother of the King of England as she proudly notes, and the charming picture of Prince William Frederick and his sister Princess Sophie passed presently into the possession of Earl Waldegrave.

In how far her personal qualities and popularity influenced her clients is not certain. Mrs. Piozzi wrote at about this time: "It is said that Painting is now little cultivated among Italians. Rome will however be the place for such inquiries, Angelica Kauffmann being settled there seems proof of their taste for living artists. If one thing more than another evinces Italian candour and true good nature, it is their generous willingness to be able to be happy in acknowledging foreign excellence."

Angelica's method of working had always been the same; she first studied her subject, read and reflected on it, and then made a preliminary sketch. This was then changed into a second sketch which was more detailed, more light and shade were added, and indications of colouring. She then studied the accessories of draperies or decoration, and finally she was ready to begin the painting. Her painting of copies had never been only for the purpose of making money, but from a desire to absorb the methods of the great masters.

17

It is time to speak of an event which was for Angelica perhaps the crowning experience in her life: her friendship with the poet Goethe. He had arrived in Rome in November 1786. This was the end of a journey of which he had dreamed through all the hazardous years of his youth. Italy—for the northerner the land of sunshine, of abundance, of the gifts of the Gods, the home of lovely women and brave men, of myth and history, of painting and of poetry! He had finished twelve arduous years in the service of Karl August, the young Grand Duke of Weimar, and had helped to make Weimar into a new Parnassus. He had written *Wilhelm Meister* and *Götz von Berlichingen* and for a time had immersed himself in scientific discovery. And now he was tired of it all, tired of his beloved Charlotte von Stein, tired of the Court, tired even of success. He had played the role of Oreste in his own *Iphigenie* and had dreamed of the character he had created, the pure unspotted virgin, all nobility, innocence and sacrifice, the matchless heroine. Now he wrote *Kennst Du das Land wo die Zitronen blühen* (Knowest thou the Land where flower the lemon groves) and *Nur wer die Sehnsucht kennt* (Only he who longing knows), the two Mignon songs, and prepared himself for flight. Goethe's latest biographer[1] tells us that Goethe possessed to an extraordinary degree the capacity to concentrate in the midst of numberless activities on the thing which was really occupying his thoughts. Thus he composed his *Iphigenie*, a poem of the deepest calm, in the midst of a recruiting foray with the Grand Duke, a dirty business as he says himself. In the contrast he may even have found a spring of inspiration as he wrote his inspired lines on the filthy

[1] Professor Richard Friedenthal.

tables of country inns surrounded by the clamour of
protesting voices.

All this was left behind. Frau von Stein had departed
for a cure to Carlsbad, and his Grand Duke on a hunting
expedition. Without a farewell, without telling anyone
where he was going, without more than a cloak and a bag,
Goethe set off to the South.

The book he wrote many years later when he was an old
man and in which he embodied many letters written on his
travels, gives a notion of what his stay of two years in Italy
had meant to him. He called it the *Italian Journey*, but it
had little resemblance to the kind of tour then so fashionable. He mixed hardly at all in high society, frequented
much more artist circles, and above all studied and did his
best to become an artist himself. He visited Milan,
Vicenza, Padua and Venice and gave the other towns he
passed through hardly a look. All his being was centred on
reaching Rome. In his own words, that longing grew
stronger every minute. Faster and faster he went, until on
1 November 1786 he arrived. Then and then only could
he calm down and look around on a scene which was so
familiar that he might have been there all his life. It must
be the experience of many a traveller to Italy who has seen
innumerable engravings, copies, casts of sculpture and the
like, to arrive, just as Goethe did, and feel immediately at
home. The names of streets, heard already in early childhood; the Forum, the Seven Hills, the Vatican with its
Galleries, all are like dear faces not seen for some time.
Once arrived, Goethe shed his feverish excitement and
made ready to enjoy his freedom. His first visit was to the
painter Tischbein, whom he knew from correspondence,
and he lost no time in unbundling the hundreds of drawings he had made on his way, for it was now his ambition
to become a painter too.

In order to be unmolested and unknown, he had assumed the name of Moeller, and Tischbein speedily found
him lodgings in a house opposite the Palazzo Rondanini
and made him free of the group of German painters then
in the city. They were all younger and poorer than he, and

they envied this wealthy aspirant who had come among
them. In fact the rumour soon went round that it was
Goethe himself, to the amusement of Tischbein who came
and told him. "This is going to be fun. The rumour that
you are already in Rome has spread and aroused the
curiosity of the artists about the only foreigner whom
nobody knows. One of our circle has always boasted of
having met you and even lived with you on terms of
intimacy, a story we found hard to believe. So we asked
him to take a look at you and resolve our doubts. He at
once declared that it was not you but a stranger without
the slightest resemblance to you. So your incognito is
preserved at least for the moment, and later we shall have
something to laugh about."

When at last they did know who he was they were amazed
at his ignorance and lack of interest in the painters whom
they most admired. Could he have passed through Padua
and Milan and not have become enthusiastic about the works
of Giotto and Leonardo? Did he really value Palladio so
highly? Great were the arguments and, since they were not
at all sure yet who he was, he records with glee that "since
they do not know who I am, they cannot talk about me. So
all they can do is to talk about themselves and the topics
which interest them. In consequence I get to know what
everyone is doing, and about everything worthwhile that is
going on." The only other person who was in the secret was
the Hofrat Reiffenstein, a valued friend of Tischbein but
also of Angelica and her husband, so it is safe to suppose
that Goethe was taken early in his stay to the house to
which every stranger to Rome desired an introduction.
Though he does not mention Angelica until much later in
his book, we know that she was amused by the "Baron-
who-lives-opposite-the-Rondanini", the name by which the
Italians distinguished the mysterious stranger. It would
have been difficult to keep away from her, for in January he
visited Father Jacquier the famous mathematician who
lived so near, on the Trinità dei Monti, whom she had
painted. And later, when he had made her acquaintance, he
would write, "It is a great pleasure to look at paintings with

Angelica, for she has a trained eye and knows a great deal about the technical side of painting. Moreover, she is sensitive to all that is true and beautiful, and incredibly modest."

It will help to have some conception of Goethe's personality at this time. He was a born romantic. The poet Auden and Elizabeth Mayer in the introduction to their admirable translation of the *Italian Journey* speak of his long devotion to Charlotte von Stein. And in the episode from the little known *Tagebuck* which Cardus re-tells in his essay *Noch einmal Wien!* the great German poet, after receiving a midnight visit from a comely but timid, waiting-girl at his inn, who had loved him at first sight and assured him that he was the first to have ever overcome her reputed coldness, left her after their night together as virginal as he had found her, a little to his chagrin—for it was he who had made the first advances when she carved the chicken for his meal with graceful movements—but consoled by the thought that "his love for his only love had won against his casual urges". It had won then. But it was not to win as he penetrated into Italy. Auden and Elizabeth Mayer write: "an artistic, somewhat bohemian, foreign colony in a great city (Rome) gave him a freedom in his personal life which would have been out of the question at a provincial German court . . . The difference between the over-refined, delicate, almost neuresthenic face of the pre-Italian portraits and the masculine, self-assured face in the portraits executed after his return is very striking; the latter is that of a man who has known sexual satisfaction."

That this is highly likely is indicated by the Faustina poems. But Goethe remained an idealist and a romantic to the end of his days and his ardent though entirely platonic relationship with Angelica reveals this clearly. By January 1787 the pretence of anonymity had been abandoned: the secret was out for Goethe had finished his play, *Iphigenie*, and had read it to his small circle; it was received with mixed feelings, its classical simplicity was not immediately understood by young men who had expected something much more in the *Sturm und Drang* style of *Götz von*

Berlichingen. But on reflection, the German colony were inclined to see more beauties than had met the immediate ear; they never stopped singing the play's praises, and a further reading was given which the Zucchis and Reiffenstein heard about. Then nothing would satisfy Angelica but that a reading should be given in her house. It was a great success and, says Goethe, even Signor Zucchi was pleased to show an unexpected interest. This evening marked the start of the intimate friendship between Angelica and the poet; it was founded on their shared devotion to the memory of Winckelmann. And at the end of February when he gave another reading of *Iphigenie*, he wrote, "Angelica, tender soul that she is, responded to my play with a sympathetic understanding that astounded me. She has promised to make a drawing based on one passage and give it to me as a souvenir. And so, just as I am leaving Rome (he was going to Naples) I have become tenderly attached to these kind-hearted people. It is both a pleasure and a pain for me to know that someone will be sorry to see me go."

For Angelica it must have been more than an ordinary leavetaking. To be in close contact with a man who, not only as a poet but as a human being, could exhibit so many strands of awareness to life and thought, was a refreshment. He saw and spoke about everything he saw with an ingenuous simplicity which was founded on a deep understanding of the springs of life; art for him as for her was not merely an occupation but an emanation from the profoundest, the most vital part of human nature, it was the breath of life; with it all he was gay, handsome, and a most excellent companion.

In February, Goethe, with his friend Tischbein, left for Naples; all these months he had spent in visiting the galleries and palaces of Rome and his reflections later in his life make exciting reading. But more than this, he had learned to record all that he had seen in the wonderful surroundings of the city, and he wrote: "The artists like giving me lessons because I am quick at understanding. Understanding is a mental faculty, but right doing requires the practice of a lifetime. However feeble his efforts may be, the amateur should not despair. The few lines I draw on the paper, often too hasty and seldom exact, help me to a better comprehension of physical objects." And elsewhere he observes, "one should draw more and talk less". Here speaks a man, so modest about his own magnificent achievements and so open to every new inspiration, who could wonder at a head of Medusa in the neighbouring Palazzo Rondanini and equally delight himself with an unfamiliar flower. He said that his youth with its eager enthusiasm had returned to him.

The brush of his new friend was being kept busy. Six portraits of young noblewomen, from paintings of their heads which Prince Poniatowsky sent from Russia, were to be combined into one family portrait, not a very easy thing to achieve with taste. Then there followed a big painting for the King of Poland representing "Augustus, Octavia and Vergil". They were surrounded by fine architecture and in the distance through one of the arches could be seen a part of the temple of Jupiter Tonans and a part of the Capitol. The price was high—330 zecchini—but it was paid the day it was sent off.

For the faithful Mr. Boydell of London, print merchant and Alderman of the City of London, she made two pictures, small life-size with scenes from Shakespeare's Comedies. One from *Two Gentlemen of Verona* and the other from *Troilus and Cressida*. These Mr. Boydell doubtless lost no time in engraving. He paid two hundred guineas.

While doing this and much else beside, she could think of Goethe's life in the colourful surroundings of Naples. There all must be movement, excitement, the life on the streets to be noted, the people in their vivid costumes, the painted carts, the carriages of the rich, the horses' harness bright with silver and gold; the noise, the singing day and night, and circling it all the improbable beauty of the bay with the ferocious mountain towering in the distance. Even the famous *lazzaroni*, Goethe remarked, were not as lazy as they were painted; they bestirred themselves from time to time, either to beg a penny or two or to do an undemanding job: that done they would curl up in a corner to sleep again, or to enjoy the crust and fruit their labour had brought them.

From this daily renewed opera-like scenario, he could escape when he wished to the house of Sir William Hamilton in Posilipo, and there admire and speculate on the incredible profusion of objects which formed the collection. For him the Etruscan and antique vases were the greatest discovery, these unvalued pieces which Sir William rescued from the excavations of Herculaneum and Pompeii, and which he brought back to his house by the basketful. And, very far from being an antique object, for she had not yet reached her majority, Goethe could feast his eyes on the beauty of Emma Hart, Sir William's so-called ward, who in her attitudes enchanted the company with a living picture of the Grecian models. Goethe described her thus:

"Sir William Hamilton who is still living here as English Ambassador, after many years of devotion to the arts and the study of nature, found the acme of these delights in the person of an English girl of twenty with a beautiful face and a perfect figure. He has had a Greek costume made for her which becomes her extremely. Dressed in this, she lets down her hair and, with a few shawls, gives so much variety to her poses, gestures, expressions, etc., that the spectator can hardly believe his eyes. He sees what thousands of artists would have liked to express realized before him in movements and surprising transformations—standing, kneeling, sitting, reclining, serious, sad, playful, ecstatic, contrite, alluring, threatening, anxious, one pose follows another without a break. She knows how to arrange the folds of her veil to match each mood, and has a hundred ways of turning it into a head-dress. The old knight idolizes her and is enthusiastic about everything she does. In her, he has found all the antiquities, all the profiles of Sicilian coins, even the Apollo Belvedere. This much is certain: as a performance it's like nothing you ever saw before in your life. We

Lady Cornelia Knight. Courtesy of the City of Manchester Art Galleries.

have already enjoyed it on two evenings. This morning Tischbein is painting her portrait."

Music too was a favourite pastime of Sir William, and the nights were fairylike in the moonlight streaming in from the lovely gardens, where the sound of song and strings flooded the rooms. But Goethe lost his artist companion here, for Sir William was planning to publish the results of his discoveries in two volumes, and he entrusted the illustration to Tischbein, who gladly agreed to aid such a generous patron.

In June, Goethe was back again in Rome and enjoying his regular Sunday morning excursions with Angelica and her husband. He noted that one of the older masters who had come into high favour at that time was Leonardo, and on one of these jaunts they had gone to see the great painting *Christ among the Pharisees* at the Aldobrandini palace. The Zucchis called for him; they drove to the palace; and then, after feasting their eyes on the masterpiece, went home to a good dinner and even better talk. He learned a great deal, he said, from seeing important works of art with these good friends, all of whom were specialists in their field, theoretical, technical or aesthetic. Hofrat Reiffenstein was also useful in another way, because when people tried to make his acquaintance he could always say he only met people introduced by the Hofrat. He was finishing *Egmont*, and discussions on this subject often occupied his conversation.

In Rome, as we have said, Goethe had for the first time in his life felt free, without bonds; and the libertine manner of life and mode of living even in the best circles, where every woman had a lover and every man a mistress, helped in this transformation. Later he was to celebrate his passion for his inamorata, a girl of the people whom he named Faustina in his poems. Now he lived in a warm, sensuous happiness hitherto unknown. Whether Angelica knew of this liaison does not appear; he would not be the first man who could live a double life, but perhaps she had become so accustomed to the local habits as to accept them. And in

9—AK * *

any case he was free; she could hardly object. He noted that his friend Tischbein had found in a convent near the Porta del Popolo a painting by Volterra which the monks were willing to sell for a thousand scudi. Poor Tischbein had no hope of raising such a sum, and Angelica came to the rescue. She paid the stipulated sum and took the painting into her house until he could afford the money. Later she bought it back from the painter for a considerably higher figure. It was a good painting, a "Deposition from the Cross", and an addition to Angelica's collection.

She and Tischbein were now both painting the poet's portrait. The latter's picture with its dramatic pose was to be very good; the likeness, everyone said, was striking and all were pleased with it. Hers was judged to be less satisfactory. "She is very disappointed," says Goethe, "it is making no progress, and is not like me. It remains the portrait of a handsome young fellow, without any resemblance whatever." It seems today, looking at the two portraits, that Goethe's verdict is unjust if understandable. Angelica painted the man she saw daily, the direct glance, the half-smiling mouth, the noble brow. Tischbein, however, painted the poet as he saw himself, romantic, with the broad hat, the cloak thrown over the shoulder and the vast Campagna stretching away behind him, "the poet's eye in a fine frenzy rolling." He also drew the poet's room in Rome with its bed and two pillows side by side, which may or may not have had its significance.

18

In July, Goethe wrote, "My present life is exactly like a youthful dream; it remains to be seen whether Fate is going to allow me to enjoy it, or whether, like other dreams it will turn out to be mere vanity." He was back in his old lodging, going out more into society, not quite so friendly with his group of young painters, but hard at work finishing his *Egmont* and hoping it would turn out well. He was rethinking his *Wilhelm Meister* too, with hundreds of new ideas in his head, but found it difficult to put things down in such a way that "each is exactly where it ought to be and not somewhere else". He brought to his friend Angelica his fourth act of *Egmont,* the end of the play where the hero, asleep in his cell the night before his execution, sees in a dream the figure of Liberty, who bears the features of his beloved Clara. She encourages him to be of good cheer, and while she signifies to him that his death will secure the freedom of the Provinces, she hails him as a conqueror and holds out to him a laurel crown. She holds the wreath suspended over his head: martial music is heard in the distance, and Egmont awakens.

Goethe came with this scene for Angelica's advice. He describes their discussion. "Today I came to Angelica and brought her my question. She had studied the play and had a copy of it. I wish you had been present," he wrote to a friend, "to have heard with what womanly tenderness she explained it all, and proceeded to analyse it. She said that everything which might have been spoken was implicit in the vision. The vision shows what was already in the spirit of the sleeping man, he could not have conveyed it better with words. How much he loved and adored Clara because she did not appear looking up to him but floated above him. Yes, it pleased her that he, who throughout his life had dreamed while awake of life and love, or rather through the joy that the thought of his beloved brought ever to his heart, now in dream lived and said to us what an exalted place she occupied." It must have been after such a talk that Angelica made her drawing of this moment in the play, and numerous other journal entries show clearly how he valued her judgement and how much his advent had contributed to her somewhat prosaic life with her down-to-earth husband. An ideal if platonic friendship was rapidly forming and it suited both of them in the circumstances.

In his life of Goethe, Hume Brown quotes a letter (since lost) from a young German artist in Rome to a friend describing a picnic which both Goethe and Tischbein and Angelica Kauffmann attended. It was made to inspect an ancient statue recently unearthed near a church on the right bank of the Tiber and the writer of the letter was proud to have Goethe playfully pinch his ear "like some great child" when he spilt some wine on the spread tablecloth in the course of the picnic. Goethe, after the company had consumed two bottles of wine, was in a relaxed mood. He maintained that the work of Michelangelo should make any other artist wish to bury pen and pencil. Tischbein reminded him that writers also had their unassailable forerunners and enquired, "What about your own *Iphigenie*?"; whereupon Goethe made a face "like a naughty boy" and left the company, to be discovered presently playing happily behind the house with a child. He had renamed her, he told them, Mignon. In the carriage on the way home, Goethe talked with such relaxed familiarity with the *vetturino* that Angelica had to give him a warning touch on the sleeve and, passing St. Peter's, Michelangelo was brought into the conversation once more when Goethe said that he felt almost in dread of him as one might feel dread in the presence of a great enchanter. Back in Rome they adjourned to an *osteria* where Goethe did full justice to the wine. The "picnic" prolonged itself till the church bells were pealing three next morning when Goethe said he must now go home to his Juno—a statue which he always called "my Juno". All this had the hallmark of a spontaneous contemporary narrative and though the letter is lost we can accept it. What the writer of the letter particularly noticed was Goethe's delicate attention to Angelica as well as the friendly attitude to all the company of one who had for ten years been a Minister of State.

That he could be considerate and painstaking comes out also in the story of how he secured for her a delicious evening of music and gaiety which she could not otherwise have had. Angelica never went to the theatre, Goethe says, and he never asked her why. But being a passionate lover of the stage he was always praising in her presence the grace and versatility of the singers and also the effectiveness of his favourite composer, Cimarosa. What he wanted above all was to share his delight with her. One thing led to another and finally his friend Bury got some of the artists to promise that they would come to his house and perform there if they were invited. But the date was never fixed until an eminent violinist from Weimar arrived in Rome. This was the opportunity they were waiting for, and it was quickly arranged. Some other friends were added to make up the audience and now came the business of making Goethe's salone fit for the festivity. They got a caterer and some decorators arranged the room, and on the appointed evening they had a brilliant concert. It was a beautiful summer night, the windows were all open and a crowd soon gathered outside to enjoy the music. Just then a carriage load of orchestral players was passing, they too stopped before the house and applauded with all their might. Then a bass voice began singing an air from the opera the musicians within were performing, all the instruments joined in, clapping came from the guests and the crowd added their efforts. Everyone was happy; never, they all declared, had any professional entertainment given so much pleasure as this one which had all happened by chance. It led to a new rumour being carried about that a rich Milord was living opposite the Rondanini, and although the evening was never repeated, Goethe could not shake off the report that he was rich and of noble birth.

There is a gap in Angelica's records for the summer of

1787 for after working on a picture for Mrs. Bryer of
London and two small ovals for Mr. Burchell, she shows no
entry until January 1788. It is to be supposed that in the
ferocious heat of the Roman summer she preferred to be at
her house at Castel Gandolfo. It was just before she left that
Goethe records one of the most revealing conversations he
ever had with her. It was after their visit to the
Aldobrandini palace and he says, "Considering her great
talent and her fortune, she is not as happy as she deserved
to be. She is tired of commissions, but her old husband
thinks it is wonderful that so much money should roll in for
what is often easy work. She would like to paint to please
herself and have more leisure to study and take pains, and
she could do exactly this. They have no children, and they
cannot even spend the interest on her capital: indeed they
could live on the money she earns every day by working
moderately hard. But she does not do anything about it and
she won't. She talks to me very frankly: I have told her my
opinion, given her advice and I try to cheer her up whenever we meet. What's the use of talking about misery and
misfortune when people who have enough of everything do
not know how to use or enjoy it? For a woman she has
extraordinary talent. One must look for what she does, not
what she fails to do. How many artists would stand the
test if they were judged only by their failings?"

This is the answer to her critics by a far greater man than
they. It gives us an insight into her character and feelings
which have until this point remained much of a mystery.
She was now a middle-aged woman who, in spite of her
remarkable success was unable to live the life of ease and
relaxation from the demands of the commercial side of her
life which she would have chosen. She had been driven hard
since her early youth. For although in England she may
have enjoyed a carefree social life, it was always conditioned
by the necessity to gain a living for herself and her father.
Now she could have had leisure, and if she had had it, her art
might have benefited enormously and have become less
stereotyped than, alas, it often was. But it would have meant
a change in her whole routine of life and would have been

unintelligible to Zucchi. It was too late for her to discard her chains and to wait patiently for the moments of high inspiration.

In September, Goethe passed some days at Frascati with Herr Reiffenstein and records, "Angelica came on Sunday to take us there; it is a paradise". Not content with a few days, in two weeks he was there again with all his friends; together they sketched, talked, argued, sang and generally enjoyed themselves. The new edition of his first four volumes of works had arrived and a leather-bound copy of *Egmont* was presented to Angelica, who promptly designed a frontispiece for it. She told its author that the poetry revealed new glories of her mother tongue to her. It could well have seemed to her that she was always in his thoughts. He turned to her for advice and approbation, and for her his friendship was a revelation of what the intimate feeling between man and woman could be. But something of an awakening was in store for her.

19

In October, they were all back in Castel Gandolfo with the summer drawing in, the weather was perfect and they could enjoy the cool mornings and evenings for walks. The wealthy Mr. Jenkins had a large magnificent villa, the Zucchis were near by, and Goethe was in his element. He had taken out his early comedy *Scherz List und Rache* and proposed to use it for a play with music; his friend Kayser from Frankfort was coming with the incidental music for *Egmont*, they could discuss it together.

Soon the company was enlarged by the addition of two ladies from Rome, a mother and daughter, where they had been his neighbours. He had never spoken to them though in Rome they had sat in front of his house in the evenings and even bowed to him after his elevation to the rank of Milord. Now in this easy society, it was a simple thing to make their acquaintance, and soon they were talking together and the poet found the daughter's "charms were enhanced by the melodious Roman dialect". A few days later, they introduced him to a very handsome young lady from Milan who was with them, and who was the sister of one of Mr. Jenkins's clerks. The two young beauties—one had light and the other dark brown hair—made a pleasant contrast, and of the two it was the Milanese who shortly engaged the poet's susceptible heart. Indeed the mother of the other rebuked him for this sudden transference of interest, explaining that such behaviour was not considered *comme il faut* in Roman society where a cavalier was expected to be faithful to his chosen one for at least a season. The Milanese had the advantage over her friend of being warmly interested in finding out about everything; she longed for knowledge, for as she said, her education had been sadly neglected. "We are not taught to write," she

The Younger Pliny and his Mother at Misenum

Courtesy of the Art Museum, Princeton University.

said, "for fear that we would use our pens to write love letters. We wouldn't even be taught to read if we did not have to read our prayer books. And nobody would dream of teaching us foreign languages." She told the poet that she saw the English papers, full of the news of all the world, lying about in Mr. Jenkins's house, and how she longed to know what they were saying. She was beautiful and at once, in the way of men, Goethe offered to teach her. The lesson was a great success; at the end, she could read a whole paragraph and he was more enchanted than ever. Now the dinner was about to begin and Angelica had arrived. She took her place and Goethe sat at her right hand. His pupil was standing behind him, and skilfully took the seat at his other side. Angelica looked somewhat surprised but said nothing. Here was *her* friend who had made such a point of avoiding *new* friends, obviously captured. He was forced to keep the conversation on a level between the two ladies, a difficult task when the one kept for the most part silence, while the other chattered away quite unrestrained, exclaiming over her lesson and the joys of speaking a foreign language.

Although she was not a main protagonist in the episode, Angelica comes so well out of the story of Goethe's sudden and passing passion for this beautiful Milanese that there is an excuse for re-telling it here. He plays the episode down in his contemporary letter to the favoured Weimar correspondents, whom he was keeping in touch with all his activities: "By the last mail, dear friends, you received no letter. The hustle and bustle of life in Castel Gandolfo, eventually became too much for me, and besides, I wanted to draw. I saw more Italians while I was there than I had seen in the whole year, and found it a pleasant experience. I became interested in a young lady from Milan who stayed for a week and distinguished herself from the ladies of Rome by her natural behaviour, common sense and good manners. Angelica was as helpful and considerate as she always is. One cannot know her without becoming her friend and one can learn a lot from her, especially how to work; it is incredible how much she accomplishes."

Goethe, however, was to suffer a cruel surprise next day.

He was looking for his friends and came upon the elder
ladies sitting in a small pavilion; courtesy obliged him to
join them for a short while, and he found himself taking
part in a subject dear to the hearts of all women—the
discussion of a trousseau. He was caught and was forced
to listen while dresses, jewels, and prospective guests
were canvassed. From there, the talk went to the merits
and demerits of the bridegroom, but who was the bride,
asked Goethe. "What, don't you know?" was the astonished reply, "who but your Milanese friend?" Next day
he went off with his wounded heart and his disappoint-
ment for an endless walk, alone with Nature. On his
return and for the rest of his stay, he was careful to
keep away from his lost beloved or only to talk to her
in the company of other people, and he emphasises that
Angelica behaved as she always did, to perfection.

Three months later, in December, Goethe writes of
"the painful thoughts" which were accompanying his
days of wonderful sight-seeing in the Eternal City and adds,

"I had learned that the fiancé of the nice young girl
from Milan had broken off his engagement—under
what pretext I did not know—and jilted her, and that
she, poor child, from shock and despair had fallen
victim to a violent fever and was in danger of her
life. Though I had no cause for self-reproach—I had
controlled my affection and stayed away from her, and
had been explicitly assured that, whatever pretexts had
been given, the *villeggiatura* was not among them—
nevertheless, I was deeply moved to think that the
dear face which I should always remember as so
friendly and happy was now clouded and changed. I
went every day to inquire how she was, twice daily at
the beginning, and it was with pain that my imagination tried to evoke the impossible and picture those
cheerful features, which deserved only sunshine and
joy, now dimmed by tears and ravaged by sickness,
their youthful bloom prematurely wasted and pale
from mental and physical suffering."

It is quite clear that Goethe himself had been the cause of the broken engagement. Mischief-makers had taken good care that the fiancé should learn that his betrothed had a new and highly talented foreign admirer; and fierce Italian pride had done the rest.

It is now that Angelica comes into the picture and, by her behaviour, shows her profound and genuine kindness of heart and how deserving she was of the sort of praise that all her friends and even mere acquaintances showered upon her. She was almost certainly a little in love with Goethe herself. It would be a strange thing if it had been otherwise. Such a feeling might easily have made a lesser woman unsympathetic or even hostile to her younger rival and the more attractive claimant to his wayward affections. But Goethe makes absolutely clear that so far from this being the case, it was Angelica who did everything in her power to lessen the severity of the blow which he had—perhaps unintentionally but certainly thoughtlessly—struck. In his retrospective review of his Italian trip, he tells how in February he was so preoccupied with noble works of art that "my spirit felt out of tune with the spirit of Carnival". He then continues:

"But for my inner and better life a most comforting experience was being prepared. In the Piazza Venezia, where some coaches stop before rejoining the moving string of the others so as to let the occupants look at the maskers going by, I caught sight of Madame Angelica's coach and went up to the carriage door to greet her. She had barely leaned out to give me a friendly nod before she drew her head in again to let me see, sitting beside her, the young Milanese, now completely recovered. I did not find her at all changed, but then, why should a healthy young person not recover quickly? Her eyes seemed even more animated and brilliant than ever and they looked into mine with a joy that went to my heart. We looked at each other for some time without speaking, until Madame Angelica broke the silence. 'I am only acting as interpreter,' she said, while her companion leaned forward to hear what she was saying, 'because my young friend cannot find words to express what she has wished and meant to say to you and has repeatedly said to me, how grateful she has been for your interest when she was ill. Her main consolation, which contributed greatly to her recovery and has enabled her to face life again, has been the sympathy shown by her friends and, in particular, by you. After those dark days of utter solitude she has found herself surrounded again by a friendly circle of good and kind people.'

" 'That is the truth!' exclaimed the girl, leaning across her friend and holding out her hand, which I could touch with mine, but not with my lips. I felt calm and happy as I stepped back into the throng of fools, and tenderly grateful to Angelica for comforting and taking care of the girl after her misfortune. She had drawn her into her most intimate circle—something which rarely happens in Rome—an action which moved me all the more because I could flatter myself that my interest in the beautiful girl had been in no small manner responsible for it."

There is a note of complacency about this last sentence which seems hardly appropriate and Friedenthal accuses Goethe of treating the whole episode "fictionally" in his retrospective notes. Goethe had "broken" a young heart and Angelica, with her customary benevolence, and perhaps with a touch of fellow-feeling, was doing her best to mend it. She was generous to Maddalena, she was generous to Goethe himself, for it was she who arranged it so that the one-time teacher could take his leave of his one-time so-much-admired pupil. Once again, when he tells this, we cannot help feeling that Goethe is unimaginative in his readiness to appear in the role of counsel for his own defence. Throughout his life, he never seems to have questioned the justification for arousing emotion and then almost as quickly beating a speedy retreat. And indeed to have been loved or admired by Goethe, even briefly, may have been an experience worth having for its own sake. In his account of the final parting from Maddalena, he describes the extinction of a flame which we are made to feel might have blazed up fiercely again at that very moment.

"My readers will hardly be surprised to hear that I did not forget to pay a farewell visit to the fair young lady from Milan. I had in the meantime often had pleasant news about her, how she had become more and more intimate with Angelica, and how well she behaved in the high society to which my friend had introduced her. I had also good reason to suppose that a well-to-do young man, a friend of the Zucchis, was not insensitive to her charms, and to hope that his intentions were serious and that he meant to declare them . . .

" . . . She spoke with tenderness of her brother and told me how happy she was to keep house for him and enable him to save something out of his modest salary to invest in a profitable business; in short, she made me quite familiar with her domestic situation. Her conversation gave me great pleasure. To tell the truth, I cut a rather strange figure, since I was compelled to relive so quickly all the details of our affectionate relationship from the first moment to the last. But then her brother entered and our farewell ended in sober prose.

"When I left the house I found my carriage but no driver and sent a boy to look for him. She looked out of a window on the mezzanine floor of their handsome house—the window was not very high up and we could easily have shaken hands. 'You see,' I called up to her, 'the Fates don't want me to go away. They seem to know that I leave you against my will.'

"What she said then and what I said in return—the course of this delightful conversation, free from all restraint, in which the inner feelings of two people who were half in love with each other were revealed—I shall not profane by repeating. Occasioned by chance, extorted by an inner need, it was a strange, laconic, final confession of an innocent and tender mutual affection, which has never faded from my soul."

20

It has been suggested that Angelica's reasons for burning Goethe's letters to her was because many of them referred to the kindly offices performed by her in this affair. Stolberg writes "that the relations between Angelica and Goethe, during his visit to Italy, require to be more clearly defined. There is no doubt that in a love episode in which the poet played the principal part, Angelica filled the role of go-between; and in consequence of this affair, before her death, she burnt any correspondence which would throw light on this or any other delicate subject." Gerard footnotes the above: "This is an allusion to a certain love episode of Goethe's with a pretty Milanese during his stay at Castel Gandolfo, which probably he did confide to Angelica, as he mentions in his diary in connection with this affair that *A* is as she always is, intelligent, good and obliging. But that such a flirtation needed a go-between, or was so serious as to necessitate the burning of his letters, is highly improbable."

Angelica had met in Rome a Goethe who had vowed himself to *Einsamkeit*—loneliness. She could not know that he had left behind in Weimar a woman with whom he had had for years the closest possible relationship, Frau von Stein, who had fulfilled a necessity of his nature, a belief in purity, in untouchable height and dignity. In the thousands of letters which he addressed to her, he called her "sister", and although they can be called lovers and he adored her, it has never been clear that their love had reached its ultimate conclusion. She was an aristocrat; she had taught him, had taken the wild, untamable youth and led him to clearer, higher ends. As he wrote, "She had dropped calm into my hot blood".

And in one of his most beautiful poems, *An den Mond*, he ends with the verse:

> Selig wer sich vor der Welt ohne Hass verschliesst
> Einen Freund im Busen hält und mit dem geniesst
> Was von Menschen nicht gewüsst, oder nicht bedacht
> Durch das Labyrinth der Brust, wandelt in der Nacht.[1]

This is what he now found again in Angelica, though over a much shorter period of time. He seldom refers to her without the words, "*Die Gute*"—the good. He loved her calm, her fastidiousness, her delicacy. She loved his youth—he was eight years younger than she—his beauty, and above all, his noble poetry. But she had not known his easily beguiled passion, his love of coquetry and inconsequential love-making. Now she had seen it, and it must have amazed her.

It seems from her accounts that she must really have spent the remainder of the year in the enjoyment of her friends; they were all together again in the city. Kayser, the musician, had arrived from Frankfort; he was busy tuning the piano, which would mean more music, and there were still excursions to the delicious surroundings of Rome. Frascati was particularly beloved by all of them. Goethe drew from Nature; Angelica relaxed, gave herself a brief rest, and conversation and conviviality were not forgotten. The poet before he left had been busy with the plans for his Weimar Duchess's visit to Rome, to which his friend Herder, the philosopher, was about to attach himself. Constant letters had to be written, apartments engaged and a host of smaller commissions looked after. January 1788 found Angelica back at her easel. Two more pictures for Prince Poniatowsky were commissioned and one, the very important one, her self-portrait, ordered by the Grand

---

[1] Happy he who without hatred leaves the world behind, and holding one friend in closest sympathy, enjoys with him all that is deeply hidden from others, or half known, and wanders through the labyrinth of consciousness in darkness.

Duke of Tuscany for his collection, which is today in the gallery of the Uffizi in Florence. It was designed as a gift for the Duke and was rewarded by the present of a gold medallion with his portrait. As well, she painted a portrait of the Prince himself in full regalia looking towards a big figure of Liberty on a pedestal with bas reliefs symbolising agriculture and commerce. A curious mixture. In the pauses from her work, she had been accustomed to take walks with her poet friend on the Palatine, where the waste spaces between the ruins of the Imperial palaces had been reclaimed and made attractive with tables and chairs, and one could be sure of other forms of entertainment besides the lovely view. They saw the great obelisk of Sesostris raised to its position on the Monte Citorio, and visited again Raphael's Cartoons which were being copied for the Empress of Russia. And then came the greatest pleasure of all, a torchlight expedition to the Museums of the Vatican and the Capitol, when they were able to see in the golden light which played upon them the works of art which in the daytime lay many of them, such as the Laocoon and a half figure of Venus, in obscure corners. On one such expedition, they and some of Goethe's artist friends had embarked on arguments which had not ended when they had crossed the river, with the result that they decided to re-cross to the further bank again. They re-crossed and the boatman's little son was heard to say, "Father, what do they want to do this for?" to which the laconic reply was, "I don't know, they're crazy". It had all meant much to Goethe and at the end of his remembrance of past times, he makes this enigmatic remark, "It was remarkable that I was forced by exterior development to take various measures resulting in new conditions, which in turn made my stay in Rome more beautiful, more useful and happier. I can say that I felt in those last weeks the highest degree of satisfaction of my life and that now I can gauge the ultimate point from which I can measure the temperature of my existence."

Before he left, he had written, "My departure will deeply sadden three people. They will never again find what they

Portrait of a Man. Courtesy of the Vorarlberger Landesmuseum, Bregenz.

had in me. It pains me to leave them. In Rome I first discovered myself, and, in harmony with myself, for the first time became a happy and a reasonable being. And as such these three have in varying senses and degree known and possessed me." Who were the three? Was Angelica one of them? We are left to guess. It must be remembered that Goethe prepared the *Italian Journey* for publication as an old man, and it would seem that after his usual fashion he used mystification to hide his real feelings and experiences. He was more interested in using this experience in Rome as another proof of his general and uninterrupted development towards his highest powers. It is significant that when he left, the thoughts of *Faust* were already in his mind. He may have amused himself by giving some account of the romantic episode of the fair Milanese to the admiring Weimar ladies. Certainly he made constant references to Angelica and acknowledged all he owed to her for advice in his artistic ventures and friendship and warmth in her distinguished home. The mysterious "Faustina" of the *Roman Elegies* was probably of humbler origin and satisfied the sensual side of his nature. Her natural, loving, animality was something he had not before encountered and she left a lasting memory of voluptuous pleasure. In Angelica he found all that he desired in goodness and intellectual beauty, the sister, the friend, always ready to understand and advise. If these were two of the three, the third remains one of those enigmas in which he loved to indulge.

Goethe's departure was a cruel blow. They had seen together their last Carnival, of which he left such a lively account, had enjoyed their last Sunday dinner and talk, had taken their last walk. They had planted in Angelica's little garden the tiny pine tree, which was to be the everlasting memory of their friendship and happy days,[1] had said their last adieux, with what a sinking of the heart one may imagine. No longer could she look forward to hearing his voice, or feeling his hand as it grasped hers in greeting, no more, no more!

[1] For a time other visitors gave him news of it. Then a newcomer to the villa uprooted it.

10—AK * *

After his departure, her first letter to him tells something of her grief.

"The tenth of May '88.

Dearest Friend—Parting from you has filled my heart and soul with grief; the day of your going was one of the most sorrowful of my life, except for the dear lines you wrote before you started and for which I have already thanked you. Now again I thank you for your letter from Florence, which I looked for with longing. A few nights ago I dreamt that I had received letters from you and that I felt consoled and said, 'It is well that he has written else I would have died of grief.'

"I am content to know that you are well; and may heaven keep you thus. I live such a sad life and because I cannot see what I most desire, all and everyone is indifferent to me, except perhaps our good friend Herr Reiffenstein, with whom I speak of you. The Sundays which were once days of joy have become the saddest days—they seem to say, we return no more! But I will not believe this, the words 'return no more' sound too hard. Now I will say not another sorrowful word. You know I have something of yours upon which you bestowed great care: I have to thank the good Schütz for this treasure. Your little pine tree stands now in my garden and is my dearest plant. One thing more I have, which I destined for you before it was mine—the figure of which I have spoken to you—the Muse. I am only waiting for a good opportunity to send it to you. You will help me in this, for it would be a thousand pities if it should suffer injury.

"I have made some alteration in the design for the title page (of *Egmont* designed by Lips)[1] also I have made it somewhat larger. I recollected that I said to you that I could myself engrave it on the copper; it is however a long time since I have done etching, and I know not how

[1] Whose chalk drawing of Goethe at the age of forty-two, though a little sterner, is strong proof that Angelica in her own portrait of the poet was not lying.

it might succeed, and the proofs would take a long time before I could be sure of success, consequently I should be glad to know if the design, which will be finished today, should be given to Herr Lips or sent to you. I await your instructions.

"In Florence you will have seen many beautiful things which you will tell me of. Zucchi thanks you heartily for your kind remembrance of him, and desires to continue in your recollection, we speak every day of you.

"Give me the only satisfaction I can now enjoy, that of hearing from you often. When I know that you are well and content I will try and reconcile myself to my fate. Farewell, my dear friend, keep me in your thoughts. Angelica."

A week later, the 17th, she is writing to him again.

"I thank you a thousand times for the joy your letter from Florence has given me. Your commission I have handed over to our good Rath Reiffenstein, and I have made your excuses to him and Abbate Spina; both love you dearly, but who can help doing that? I am not at all pleased with Herr Kayser, he has left you very much alone and evidently prefers the library to your company. Ah, if I were in his place! And how I envy him. It is true that I am often as near you as your own shadow, but let the power of imagination be ever so strong, it yet remains only imagination . . . I forget what has happened since you left. When I think of you I grow confused. I sit with the pen in my hand, have much to say, would wish to say much to you—every pulse of my heart suffers and complains. But of what use is all this? Nothing I can say will bring you back to me. It were better that I remained silent; your feeling heart can imagine the rest. Since the 23rd, that last and fatal day—I have been in a dream out of which I cannot rouse myself—the lovely sky, the most lovely scenery, alas, even the divine in Art excites nothing in me—I am indifferent to all. I really believe that I am on the outer edge of that folly of which we often talked.[1] In the other world I hope it will be arranged that all dear friends meet never more to part, and so I look for a happier life above . . .

"Your *Tasso* will be received by me with love and joy, it is joining new links to the chain, nevertheless every word you have written is precious to me because it is yours."

Are these the letters of a mere friend, even allowing for the exaggerated sentimentality of the time? We think not. Such an agony breathes from them, her feelings must seem so authentic to anyone who has ever suffered parting and loss that it is clear that Angelica, however much she disguised the fact from herself while he was there, loved the poet deeply, agonisingly. She tried to comfort herself with the thought that he would return, that his letters would be a solace, in her heart she knew that it was not true; he was gone. The black bitter cloud came over her, her whole being mourned, and she must turn a calm face to the world and go on with her work. For that was all that was left to her.

She wrote him little pieces of news; a portrait of Lady Hervey and that of Cardinal Rezzonico were finished and she was considering the one for the Czarina. It would be Achilles. And her picture for the Grand Duke had been accepted. She thanks him for some sketches of his travels, and here feeling once more breaks through. "Now that I have them I find my thoughts are very often there. Rome is beautiful, but no more so for me. Let me be still, let me once more be master of my pen." It is wrung from her suffering heart. But the poet felt no such twinges; he had paid an affectionate farewell to the young lady from Milan who had so charmed him and was off "to fresh fields and pastures new", to Weimar where further triumphs of love and applause awaited him. He wrote a few letters. He was done with painting and had bought himself a hammer with which to collect specimens of rocks. He was done with platonics and it would not be long before Christiane

---

[1] Was this suicide? As a pious Catholic, Angelica can hardly have contemplated that.

Vulpius—whom he eventually married—would be installed in his garden-house. Women might come and go. One was useful to him, many were mere pleasure, none would ever again give him quite the measure of support which Charlotte von Stein and Angelica had done. But all that was past and when, later, the Duke required Goethe to meet the Duchess Amalia in Italy and escort her home, he stipulated that he would go no further than Venice.

21

In September 1788 came a regular flood of German visitors from Weimar all set aflame to visit Rome by Goethe's descriptions of the city. First came Herder, accompanied by Frau von Seckendorf. Naturally his first visit was to the wonderful artist of whom Goethe had spoken so often and so glowingly. On 21 September she wrote to the latter:

"On the 19th of this month when I came home at my usual hour I found Bury in the drawing room with Herr Herder. It gave me joy to see this excellent man, your friend. I gave him your letter, the questions about which you are anxious he could scarcely answer since he is only just arrived. The visit was short but he has given me the hope that he will come often. The Duchess Mother will arrive at the end of the month. You know already, my dear friend, how much I wish to do honour to those whom you like and to be of use to them if I can; it rejoiced me that they have come at a time to enjoy the neighbourhood. It will soon be the season when we were together at Castel Gandolfo—every place where you sketched will be dear to me, all will remind me of what is past, and with such a memory I can hope for enjoyment in the present. In my imagination I will see you everywhere. We shall spend only a few days there this year as we intend to make a short tour in October. You console me with a hope for the future. I will try and hope for the best, it may make the present more bearable. That my little offering"—she means the sculptured Muse which she had sent him— "which you so kindly accepted, should have arrived at a time and on a day which shall be forever sacred to me, this coincidence makes me happy, may I live to keep that day with you again. 'Tis Sunday and instead of going to fetch

you I am writing these few lines with the little pen I stole
from you ... I have seen Herr Herder again; what a
worthy man he is, and speaks as he writes. We showed
him your bust which pleases your friend much.[1] I am
content with the likeness. When I wanted to pay Herr
Trippel my debt, he said you had paid him, consequently
I have to thank you infinitely for such a dear present. I
spend many minutes in the day looking at it ... The
drawing room is arranged: Daniel Volterra in his case is
placed where the great architectural picture by Zucchi
used to hang. This same picture serves as the decoration of
the salon, in the middle of which Mercury is placed for
light ... The garden has produced nothing wonderful
this year. The dear pine grows, I have not transplanted it.
You would laugh at my anxiety when the sky is darkened
by clouds and when there are signs of a storm. I run into
the garden, and place the young plant under cover for fear
it might be injured; all the rest I leave to their fate."

She adds,

"I hear *Tasso* has advanced very far towards completion
as also another work which you have of which you have
said nothing to me. I remember the happy times when
you read me your manuscripts: these days will never, I
fear, come again; the very thought fills me with sadness."

In December Herder dined for the first time in
Angelica's house and by this time he was a welcome guest
whenever she was free. He wrote "She is a fine soul,
delicate and sincere, altogether the artist, without physical
charm, but very interesting in every way. Her most striking
qualities are simplicity, sincerity and sensitivity. It is a sad
thing for humanity that she is ageing somewhat. She gave
me a very friendly welcome, but I did not stay long."
Herder put his finger on Angelica's weakness; it was her
misfortune always to give the impression of simplicity,
impeccability, utterly unsensual, not the qualities which
appeal superficially to men. After the dinner, at which

[1] This bust had been made by the sculptor Trippel and presented to the
Zucchis.

Angelica appeared as the perfect hostess, he wrote to his wife in Hamburg. "She is a fine womanly soul like a Madonna or a little dove. In a small gathering of two or three she is altogether delightful. But she lives so quietly, in a painter's world of ideas, like a small bird which only pecks at fruit or flowers with its beak." He goes on to say that her old husband seemed to be like an old Venetian in a comedy; in fact everything seemed like a scene in a comedy.

Almost immediately after the Duchess arrived with an immense suite. She came with the reputation of a protectress of all the arts; it was largely her doing that Weimar was styled the new Athens. Her advent was hailed by all and she speedily attracted a circle of the most eminent people in Rome. The Pope, cardinals, bishops, ambassadors, Italian and foreign nobles, savants, artists and musicians, all came to her door and yet she herself preserved an unspoilt air, a general interest in all that was best. Soon Angelica was painting her portrait, and in the intimacy of the sittings the two women became close friends; drawn together at first by their admiration for Goethe, they found in each other a common love of beauty and in intellectual pleasure. They could have said with Wordsworth, "I have felt a presence that disturbs me with the joy of elevated thoughts". The Duchess wrote to Goethe: "I go to see Angelica as often as I can, and she comes to see me; she is in every way a lovable woman. Next Friday I am to sit to her for my portrait, certainly not as a model, but I wish to have something of hers. Old Zucchi has given me some of her drawings."

But Angelica's first letter is in a more enthusiastic spirit.

"Do you know, my dear friend, that I am coming to Weimar; have you ever dreamed of such a thing? Her Excellency the Duchess has invited, in the most cordial way, good Rath Reiffenstein, Zucchi and me to accompany her back or to follow her. Fraulein von Goechhausen and Herder were present and added their entreaties. Was it possible to refuse such a gracious proposal? The promise has been given if circumstances permit it. Blessed Weimar, which since it has given me the joy of knowing you I have so often envied, where my thoughts fly constantly, shall I really see it and see YOU there? Oh most beautiful dream, and still I hope that even before this journey comes off we may see you in Rome. That the Duchess has shown herself so gracious to me I have to thank you, my best and dear friend."

She goes on to describe a charming evening spent together in the Capitoline Museum and when in the hall of the Muses, Herder proposed they should each offer a prayer to the god, her prayer to Apollo was that he would inspire Goethe to return to Rome. Unfortunate Angelica! the god was perhaps "asleep or on a journey", for her prayer remained unanswered and, as we have said, when it was time for the Duchess's party to return to Weimar, he came only as far as Venice to meet her.

She painted on, perhaps finding in her work a satisfaction which could dull her pain. She finished two Shakespearean pictures for Mr. Boydell of London, the Duchess's portrait was done and the Lady wrote to Goethe that it had seemed to grow under the painter's fingers, though privately and later she did not think so much of it. But their evenings together were cheerful. Herder read Goethe's poems, perhaps Angelica sang and played for them, and soon it was time for the royal party to depart for a visit to Naples, and Angelica wrote to her friend that the Duchess had taken the villa which was next to a garden they had shared, did he remember it? And why, oh *why* was he not there, why did he keep away from Rome? On 23 May 1789 she wrote that the party had left the city.

"I must acknowledge that I was happy when I had so many of your friends near me. We spoke so constantly of you and the Duchess showed herself always so extremely gracious towards me: her suite too were full of kindness. On the 19th her Excellency left for Naples to spend the summer. It seems to me now that I have been in a dream of pleasant companionship, and have just awakened to resume my solitary life again. Also the good, excellent Herder is gone. This day fortnight I spent with the

distinguished Society at Tivoli at the Villa d'Este; under
the great cypress trees, Herder read to us the part of *Tasso*
which you have sent. I cannot tell you with what pleasure
I listened. I think of all your works it is the most beautiful.
Who can read such a masterpiece and not long to hear the
rest? Herr Herder gave me the manuscript for which I
thank you warmly.

"For a long time I have been intending to write and
thank you for the eight volumes of your work which you
sent me (he had given her this present so that she might
'renew her acquaintance with her native language'). I delayed because I feared you would say that I wrote too often."

She was evidently feeling that her beloved friend had
changed since he left. Gone were the long intimate talks; she
feared to molest him by seeming too insistent, and she
assures him that she would honour him and his friendship as
long as she lived. "I can only say that I live and hope to live
in *your* memory as you do in mine, where the remembrance of
you will always and forever be dear."

Is it possible that Angelica recognised herself in the figure
of Leonora, the real heroine of the poet's play? In this noble,
self-sacrificing woman, Goethe embodied his notion of the
heroic feminine the picture is of course romanticised, but
Leonora stands there as the embodiment of all that is best in
the feminine nature, the ideal which the poet needed for one
side of his dualistic self. So had Frau von Stein stood, and so
she expected to stand when he returned, but was to be sadly
disillusioned. He indicated in very plain terms when he got
back that all his earlier life had been left behind. He knew
now his true path, he was to be the "Universal Man", poet,
scientist, political counsellor, who would honour with his
presence the small but distinguished Weimar. And it did not
take long either before he had made provision with the aid of
the garden-house for the satisfaction of the more sensual side
of his nature.

What chance had Angelica, with her despairing cry,
"Why do you not return to Rome? Why? Why?" In August
she wrote,

"Oh that for once I could see you all together, and spend the evening with you. Rome, now that I am losing all my friends, is fast becoming a desert. Paintings and statues are beautiful to look at, but to be surrounded by friends is better; these are the thoughts I dwell on, they disturb my rest and sadden my heart. I try to occupy myself as much as possible so that the hours slip away unnoticed until a better time comes. May you always be happy and well, and grant me sometimes the happiness of a few lines. The pine is in full growth, so also are the other plants which you brought out of the Botanical Garden. Once more I recommend myself to you, my honoured friend, and remain always, with great esteem."

She sent him a title page for *Tasso*, and with it their correspondence seems almost to have ended. Although it is out of context, we may include one last letter from Goethe, written on 25 June 1797. It begins coldly enough: "The hope I had entertained, most honoured friend, of seeing you in the coming year, is, through this most miserable war, at an end, as the way to Rome is completely barred, at least for the present." He has a favour to ask her. A friend of his wants to make a catalogue of her paintings and he believes that she could furnish a copy of one made by Zucchi. He goes on to say, "Not many days ago your excellent picture of 'Cupid and Psyche', which I saw in Dessau, gave me the most exquisite pleasure. You cannot conceive the impression these heavenly creatures make, when seen amidst the snowflakes of the icy north, which are only suited to a wild beast or a dull huntsman ... The excellent likeness which you painted of our Duchess, which I believe is to be placed in a new summer palace just built by the Duke, has somewhat changed its appearance, the cause, I imagine, being that the varnish has either flown or sunk into the picture, so that the brightness of the colouring and the harmony of the whole is manifestly injured. It will be easy, by means of revarnishing, to restore the portrait to its original freshness, but I am afraid lest a wrong varnish ignorantly applied might do more harm than good, and irretrievably ruin the work. Will you, therefore, have the kindness to tell me what varnish I should use, and what medium I should employ to secure it?" The letter concludes as formally as it began: "Farewell, and kindly answer yourself or through others. Goethe."

So Angelica was left with her art, and for the moment with a new and increasingly ardent admirer, the philosopher Herder, who for all his analytical mind, does not seem to have had the slightest conception of what had been passing in Angelica's heart. His German sentimentalism was enchanted by this pure soul, "this angelic and childlike innocent". The adulatory letters he wrote to his wife on the subject would be funny if they were not so sincere. But even he found it advisable to inform his spouse left behind in Weimar that Angelica was not at all attractive to him physically. Frau Herder responded with the utmost tact and patience to all her husband's effusions, and Angelica too seems to have found comfort in the adoration and respect which this very eminent man of letters felt for her. She sent friendly notes to the absent wife and the present of a ring and Frau Herder seems to have taken it all in good part until her husband's rhapsodies on the subject of his new friend appeared to be getting out of hand. He wrote:

"She is indeed an angel of a woman, and her goodness sets the balance between me and others of her sex who have done me bad turns. She has the activity of a man, and has done more than fifty men would have done in the time. In goodness of heart she is a celestial being. I gave her your kiss as it stood in your letter, *without transferring it to her lips.* Once I did kiss her on the forehead, and once she unexpectedly seized my hand and would press it to her lips. *There,* that is all between us. I thank my God that He made me to know this pure soul, and that through her I carry away one pleasant memory of Rome ... You must love Angelica for my sake for she deserves it, the strangely tender loving soul; she knows thee, and we speak of thee often, and then she says so softly she believes thee to be very happy ... Take the letter she sends thee kindly; she is not strong in words, but in deeds a most honest soul."

It may have been this letter which prompted Madame Herder to write that she felt like Ariadne deserted by Theseus, and to urge him to return home with all possible speed. It was Angelica's fate to inspire poets with the noblest sentiments, she seems either to have been a thorough-paced sentimentalist herself, or else to have had an unequalled capacity for giving men the sort of sentimental companionship they craved.

In any case the plan to visit Weimar had collapsed, whether because it had not been encouraged by Goethe or because of her old husband's stinginess. It suited him better to keep his wife in Rome earning money. And this she was doing. She noted, on the last day of August 1789 that the total sum of payment for pictures done in Italy from October 1781 was 14,690 zechins, and in October came a very important commission, one of her infrequent holy pictures. It was for the chapel of Bartolomeo Colleoni at Bergamo by order of the Cardinal Carrara, a picture a little less than life size, representing the Holy Family, the Virgin and the Holy Child, St. John with the lamb and St. Joseph. It was finished and sent off in May 1790, and still hangs in the chapel. Now came an even more important undertaking, a picture for the Empress of all the Russias, life size figures representing Achilles being discovered whilst disguised in feminine attire; he is with the maidens of Deidamia, daughter of King Lycomedes. In a letter to a friend, she said that it presented a formidable task.

In the autumn of 1789 she received a visit from a fellow-artist of her own sex. This was the French painter Madame Vigée le Brun: she too had been a youthful prodigy and in the course of her travels now had been particularly curious in Florence to see the portrait of Angelica, "one of the glories of our sex". The two women had much to tell each other and, in a letter to Hubert Robert, le Brun describes their meeting. "I have been to see Angelica Kauffmann whom I had a great desire to know," she wrote. "I found her very interesting, apart from her talents, on account of her intelligence and her knowledge. She is a woman of about fifty,[1] very delicate, her

---

[1] Actually she was forty-eight.

health having suffered in consequence of her marriage in the
first instance with an adventurer who had ruined her. She has
since been married again to an architect who manages her
affairs for her. We had much excellent talk together during
the two evenings I spent at her house. Her conversation is
agreeable, *elle a prodigeusement d'instruction, mais aucun
enthousiasme, ce qui, vu mon peu de savoir, ne m'a point elec-
trisée.*" It may be for this reason that Madame le Brun, who
was a most lively painter, was content with the two evenings
spent with Angelica. And it is likely that Madame le Brun
did most of the talking, for she could tell a painter, living in
the midst of a world as yet unmoved by the events in France,
of her own escape and the horrors she had seen. In 1789, the
Bastille had fallen and panic had ensued. Aristocrats who
were friends of the King and Queen, had left the country,
and Louis XVI was engaged in a struggle to keep what was
left of the monarchy intact. But as yet the outer world,
though distressed, had not realised the full impact of
events.

In February 1790 came news from Vienna of the
Emperor's death. Joseph II had been an enthusiastic patron
and Angelica must have felt a lively regret. But it also meant
the translation of another patron, the Grand Duke Leopold,
to be the new Emperor. He inherited a country at war with
Turkey and with the Low Countries in a state of insurrection. His Coronation at Frankfort was however none the less
glorious for all that, and he proceeded to lesser festivities at
Buda Pest and Prague. For the latter, the States of Bohemia
wished to celebrate the occasion with a brand new opera and
they therefore commissioned Mozart to write an opera in the
fashionable classical style. The composer, who was deeply
engaged with work on his *Requiem*, took an old libretto by
Metastasio, *La Clemenza di Tito*, and though he had been
given but two months in which to produce the work, he had
it ready in this incredibly short time. It was his last opera; in
a few months he was dead. It fell very flat on its first
performance, in an evening show before an audience which
had during the day endured all the rigours of a long

coronation ceremony, and the new Empress was heard to murmur that she hated this *Porcheria di musica tedesca*.[1]

Later in 1790, Angelica painted a legendary figure, Frederick Harvey, fourth Earl of Bristol and Bishop of Cloyne and Derry. This fantastic and eccentric personage, who loved to drive through Rome in eccentric attire and drawn by six horses, was enormously wealthy. He had been one of the enlightened peers who had opposed the Union, and had with his friend, Lord Charlemont, helped to found the Volunteers in Ireland. A supporter of the arts, a lover of architecture, a lawyer and agriculturist, he now spent most of his time in Rome, not even returning to England when ordered by the King. He was an omnivorous reader and collector and his new house at Ickworth was designed to house his Italian treasures. He was devoted to food and to the opposite sex, and, in fact, a very unsuitable holder of a bishopric. But he got on splendidly with Angelica who painted an extremely good picture of him sitting next a pedestal with a bust of Maecenas on it. It was handed to the Irish painter, More, to be sent to England, and paid for by the banker Torlonia with 258 Roman crowns. It can be seen today at Ickworth. She painted also for the Princess of Holstein-Beck a self portrait, herself deciding between painting and music. This may have been the one now in the collection of Lord St. Oswald, or she may have painted two versions of the subject.

The news from France was becoming increasingly ominous. A new Constitution had been extorted from the King, Louis XVI; and Queen Maria Carolina had commented, "The King of France having accepted and signed what was imposed on him has finished playing his part. All sovereigns will have to do likewise sooner or later; that is my conviction." Like her sister, Marie Antoinette, she was gifted with a long-sighted estimate of history. The King's elderly aunts had appeared in Rome and now were demanding asylum in the palace at Caserta, greatly to Maria Carolina's disgust.

In December 1791, Angelica received an exceedingly

[1] This pig-wash of German music.

interesting commission, no less than to paint the portrait of
the great love of Nelson's life, Lady Hamilton, the former
Emma Hart, mistress of Sir William Hamilton who, after
five years of life together, had finally married her. The
records of Manners and Williamson tell us, "With reference
to the picture of Lady Hamilton, an exceedingly important
letter addressed by Angelica Kauffmann to her came recently
to light. It would appear from it that the picture painted in
1791 either disappeared for a while, or was a very long time
in reaching its destination, and apparently it had only been
found just before this letter was written, 31 December
1793." In the course of the letter, Angelica says,
"Tomorrow a new year begins, may it be happy to you, My
Lady, with numberless years to come, may Heaven bestow
every blessing on you and *those who are dear to you*." Manners
and Williamson comment: "The underlined words in its
penultimate sentence perhaps refer to Sir William Hamilton,
whose wife Lady Hamilton had become some two years
before; but their strange reticence and the manner in which
they are underlined give to them unusual importance and
lead us to wonder whether they formed a cryptic allusion to
new lovers who had just come upon the scene. This allusion
is not to Lord Nelson, who certainly was in the
Mediterranean in 1793, but whose friendship with the
famous beauty did not commence till September 1798, when
he reached Naples fresh from his victory at Aboukir. The
curious word Gadeghan in the postscript is probably a
phonetic spelling of Cadogan and in that case it refers to
Lady Hamilton's mother, who had assumed the name of
Mrs. Cadogan."

This picture of Lady Hamilton as the Muse of Comedy is
one of Angelica's most beautiful. She is shown lifting up a
curtain as if just appearing before the public while with the
other hand she is holding a mask; she is garbed in classical
style. We know that this was the lovely Emma's favourite
portrait; she kept it always with her, and when some of her
beauty faded it could remind her of those marvellous days in
Naples when she charmed everyone who knew her. There is
also in existence a very beautiful drawing in black chalk by

Captain Robert Dalrymple. Courtesy of the Earl of Stair.

Angelica of the head of Lady Hamilton, clustered with curls and slightly inclined to one side. This drawing at one time belonged to Lord Northwick.

Miss Gerard states that the oil-painting was the cause of a quarrel between the artist and a celebrated Italian engraver, Wilhelm Morghen, who in his reproduction of it changed some part of the original.[1] This infuriated Angelica and she would not allow her name to be put to it.

In 1791 Angelica sent to the Exhibition of the Royal Academy two pictures. She had not sent pictures for many years, and may have been inspired to do so by a comment of Fanny Burney some time before. "Colonel Goldworthy has just sent me in a newspaper, containing intelligence that Angelica Kauffmann is making drawings from "Evelina" for the Empress of Russia. Do you think the Empress of Russia hears of anything now besides Turkey and the Emperor? And is not Angelica Kauffmann dead? Oh, what an Oracle. For such is the newspaper called."

The reporter in the paper had gone on to say that Angelica Kauffmann in Rome was said to have finished three drawings from Miss Burney's "Evelina", Mr. Pratt's "Emma Corbett" and Miss Lee's "Recess". She was also engaged on some historic pieces for the Empress of Russia, as were these drawings. One can understand Miss Burney's annoyance, but not her ignorance of the fact that even in time of war the arts were not neglected by imperial admirers. By exhibiting once more at the Academy, Madame Angelica could not have said more clearly, "My dear Miss Burney, I am not dead, far from it!"

In 1792, Angelica had various important commissions. For a Baron de Meerman, a Dutch aristocrat, she painted a picture which she must have enjoyed working at, for it embodied two very pretty young women friends whom she painted for her own pleasure; they figured as the Muses in a life-size group. The one was the daughter of Mr. Giovanni Volpato, a celebrated engraver, and the other the wife of Mr. Raphael Morghen, another eminent engraver. This would

[1] His brother Raphael later did exactly the same thing and it was equally resented.

show that the quarrel that she had had with him earlier was
made up.

In 1792 Leopold, the recently-crowned Emperor, died
suddenly, and Angelica could not have been unmoved by the
death of her royal patron, particularly since all Europe was
thrown into confusion. He was succeeded by his brother
Francis, and Maria Carolina's daughter was now Empress.
In April 1792, while Angelica was painting for Baron de
Meerman, France had declared war on Austria, and the
French King and Queen were imploring help from any and
every side. Gustav of Sweden was ready to lead a crusade on
their behalf, and in her rage and grief the Queen of Naples
would have been glad to follow his lead. But Naples had a
thriving trade with France; discretion prevailed. The new
French government replaced Talleyrand, the late ambassador, by another representative, whom the Queen, choked
with animosity, was forced to receive. His name was de
Bassville.

But still people travelled and still they commissioned
pictures, and the year 1793 saw many new English clients.
There were two English ladies of good family but in
straitened means now living in Rome, Lady Knight and her
daughter Cornelia, the latter an authoress whose books were
much admired by no less a judge than Horace Walpole.
Although not rich, they knew everybody and went everywhere, and Lady Knight's letters to her friends in England
provide an intimate account of the passing scene. She loved
the Italians but loathed the French, for whom she had not a
good word to say, especially now when war had been
declared between them and England. On 23 August 1793,
she wrote: "We are now very tranquil in Rome and I think it
is but just to say of this Court that it has acted with the
greatest candour and vigour and at the same time with the
greatest humanity to the distressed clergy (the French exiled
priests who had refused to take the oath to the revolutionary
government). At present everybody is anxious about the fate
of the Queen of France . . . I don't know whether I ever told
you about Madame Angelica whom we knew in England,
and who resides here. We have always been very intimate

with her: she often desired us to give her leave to paint my Cornelia, but we declined, my purse not being of length sufficient to pay her for the time she not only has the power of making good use of, but the money she gains by it. However at length it has been consented to. Cornelia is drawn at half length, seated with her pencil in her hand, books beside her, and the beginning of a column for the first naval victory. She is dressed in white, with a purple mantle, and a purple ribbon round her head. On her girdle Madame Angelica had placed a cameo of Minerva, but we got her to alter it, and put in a medallion of Angelica, a head lettered with her name. Famous as she is in all she does, yet this is said to be the very best portrait she ever painted and pleases everybody. To say the truth it gives me great pleasure for it's very like Cornelia and expresses the good sense she really has."

Another fervent admirer of Angelica was in Rome at this time—Mr. Parker, later to be Lord Morley, the owner of Saltram, which ancestral seat he was in process of altering with the expert aid of Robert Adam. This magnificent example of the good taste of the time houses today, among its priceless collection of treasures, no less than eleven of Angelica's best works, both classical and historical; and not only these but her portrait of Sir Joshua Reynolds and one of Mr. Parker himself. In the dining room, which shows Robert Adam in his happiest mood, stand two splendid urns in the classical style, both with decorations by Angelica, and inset in a side table is a delicious small painting also by her, while on the delicate green and white walls hang pictures by Zucchi, Robert Adam's favourite collaborator.

His Royal Highness Prince Augustus was also in Rome. All the English who were in the city pursued him and Lady Knight remarks on their propensity for late hours, card playing and clustering together. However, the lady may have been biased for she was not gregarious herself and her daughter was a Blue Stocking, spoke ten languages and wrote serious books, all gifts which were not calculated to appeal to the more eligible of the gilded Milords who filled the city.

It was a very prolific year for Angelica. Another picture was for the young Lord Berwick who was travelling in Italy with his mother and sisters. It represented Venus sitting on a couch playing with Cupid who is smiling at having wounded Euphrosine's hand with one of his arrows. Euphrosine is grieving about it, and showing Venus her hand. Dr. John Clarke, who was travelling with the party in the character of tutor, mentions in the life of his patron that "Lord Berwick is employing Angelica Kauffmann in painting, and I am now selecting passages from the poets for her to paint for his house at Attingham". Both these pictures still hang in this house. For Mr. Bowles she painted four small pictures, all classical subjects; and, for Signora Bandettini of Lucca, another poetess and "a wonderful improviser and a member of the Arcadian Society, whose *nom de plume* is Amaryllis", her portrait attired as a Muse and wearing a crown of ivy leaves.

Presently news came that the French Queen was dead. The Revolution was in full swing, and it was not without its repercussions in Italy. The rulers in all the neighbouring states hated the Revolution, but they were nevertheless divided in their plans to oppose its results, which were already being felt in their domains. The proposals of the Tuscan Grand Duke for a combination of neutrals in 1792 had been rejected, and as a result the French armies occupied Savoy and annexed Nice in January 1793. Sardinia had also been attacked by the French fleet, but was successful in repulsing it. In Rome things were somewhat different; relations between the Papal government and France had already been broken off before the Declaration of the Republic, on account of the ecclesiastical laws of the Constituent Assembly demanding that all priests should take a civil oath; and, in January 1793, the quarrel was still further exacerbated by the murder of the French diplomat De Bassville. He had been actively engaged in fomenting trouble and inciting the populace to revolt against their rulers. But apart from this isolated act, Rome, as Lady Knight said, was tranquil and people went about their own business. In Naples, as may be readily imagined, things were different. The Queen had followed her sister's increasing danger with an equally increasing horror and the end when it came prostrated her totally. She had written, "I do not know what to hope or fear for her and her family. What I wish is that France could be crushed to powder and all its inhabitants." When the news came, she led her children to the palace chapel, where they added their prayers and tears to hers. And under a picture of her sister she wrote, "*Je pouruiverai ma vengeance jusqu'au tombeau.*" (I will pursue my vengeance until the tomb.) But what could she do? Her kingdom was full of Neapolitan Jacobins, conspiratorial clubs proliferated and the mourning for the dead monarchs was only observed by the Court and the Royalists.

What effect any of this had on Angelica we can only surmise. No doubt she too was horrified. As a devout Catholic she would deplore the hatred of religion by the republicans. And as a person who was dependent on aristocratic patrons she would hate the new State. But her work was her chief concern. The admirers of her art did not fail her. She painted in 1794 for Mr. Henry Benton, whom she mistakenly calls an English nobleman, a picture of his wife as a Muse richly attired and holding in her hand a piece of paper on which are written some lines of music. Lord Grandison likewise commissioned a portrait of Lady Gertrude Villiers, his daughter, and Lord Hervey an oval size head on canvas, his own portrait, as well as a copy of the half-length size portrait of Angelica herself by Sir Joshua Reynolds.

Lord Berwick next desired a large picture with figures representing Ariadne deserted by Theseus. She is on a richly adorned rock by the seashore and is weeping. Bacchus has been led to her by Cupid, who by lifting a fold of the rich material which forms a sort of pavilion shows to Bacchus the disconsolate Ariadne. And about this time, she made a gift to the sitter of a life size head of Signor Giovanni Volpato, her friend the celebrated engraver. All such gifts serve to show us something of the circle in which Angelica lived and with whom she had close connection. Without exception they were people of outstanding talent and intelligence, lovers of poetry and the fine arts, who could appreciate with her the pleasures of music and conversation.

Many of her clients of course were on a different footing.

They were often wealthy people who wished to decorate their
houses with works by the artist most in fashion or to take as a
souvenir of a stay in Italy some pleasing memento. It was
they who brought in the zecchini on which Zucchi was so
intent. Lord Plymouth, for example, paid a high price for the
portrait of his two children, painted as Love and Psyche.

Her domestic situation was changing. Already in 1790,
Zucchi had been showing signs of approaching old age; he
could no longer fulfil his duties as guardian of her interests,
and generally help in her affairs, so leaving her free to do her
own work. Feeling this, he had invited a young relative of
hers, Anton Joseph Kauffmann from Schwarzenberg, to
join the household, and this arrangement proved most bene-
ficial to both of them. Europe was unsettled and, by 1795,
the visitors to Rome were diminishing. The English were
the last swallows of a late summer, and the central Europeans
and Russians had almost gone. She painted two pictures for
the Princesses Esterhazy but they were small and only
brought 60 zecchins each. And then a portrait of Maddaleno
Volpato of Milan, born Riggi, Goethe's beloved, who had
married the engraver and with whom she had always kept in
friendly correspondence. Indeed it was almost certainly
through her that they had met and she could now depict
her friend as a handsome, finely built, voluptuous-looking
Milanese matron and not the fevered, love-sick maiden of
Goethe's narrative.

For his Royal Highness Prince Augustus Frederick of
England she made another fine painting, a full-length portrait in which he is wearing the Scots Highland military
uniform. Beside him, as he stands, is a white greyhound: a
good picture, with, in the background, a mountainous landscape. This is the last entry in her meticulous record of
pictures painted since her arrival in Rome. Hereafter there
are only loose leaves pasted in, a sure sign of the disturbance
of mind in which she was living, for we know her as a most
orderly and conscientious person. To the anxieties of the
time had been added her fears for her husband's health. He
had been ailing for some time, one of his hands was partially
paralysed so that he could no longer control his brush, and,

deprived of the possibility of work, he became querulous, as most semi-invalids do. He wanted to sell the house he owned in John Street, London for there began to be great uncertainty as to whether the English government which was at war with France could let interest or other monies out of the country. Zucchi also wanted assurance about various sums owed to him by Sir Rowland Winn, the owner of Nostell Park. His gloom over the whole situation deepened and, in January 1795, he died of an attack of jaundice. Contrary to the expectations of most people, Angelica was shattered, but this seems understandable. Her companion was gone, the one who had made life easy for her, who understood her whims, who entered into her happiness, gloried in her fame, and sorrowed with her sadness. He was not a romantic hero, but a good reliable staff on which to lean.[1] And he must have been a kind man, for on his tomb she wrote, "To my sweetest kindest husband, Not as I had prayed." What had she prayed for? Not to be left alone? For some fulfilment in life that had been denied to her? We don't know. We can only speculate. And she will never tell us. She was left with a worsening situation in her affairs which he had looked after so carefully. And he had not added to her tranquillity, for he had left her a miserable pittance—fifteen pounds a year in short annuities. All the rest of his property was devised to his brother and nephew. Perhaps the will had been made when Angelica's affairs were flourishing, and when Goethe had wondered why the couple should work so hard when they had no children and no financial anxieties.

She showed no resentment over the will when she wrote to their solicitors in London thanking them for their punctuality and attention and acknowledging the receipt of some relatively small sum.

". . . I daresay ye have before now read my last, written in January, I forget the date, by which letter I announced to you my misfortune, the irreparable loss I sustained by the death of my worthy husband, friend and best

[1] After his death the careful list of her pictures ceased as if it was Zucchi who had always insisted on this meticulous record of pictures and prices being kept.

companion, but such was the will of God to which we must submit. I find in your last favour that the affair about disposing of the house is still in agitation. What is done in that is now the business of Mr. Zucchi's heirs in Venice; perhaps it will be necessary to inform them what steps are necessary they should come into possession of what was left to them by my deceased husband. To me he has left only the half interest of his short annuity, the other half goes to his nephew. What I must do to come into possession of my little share ye will be so good as to tell me, as I am totally ignorant about these matters and melancholy affairs.

"I am glad to hear from you that all the pictures arrived safely to their destination . . . I repeat my thanks for all your kindness and remain gentlemen, Your most obliged servant.

Angelica Kauffman-Z."

She sent a further letter a few days later in which she once more points out that they should work directly with the Zucchis and once more explicitly says that she approves of all that her husband has done for them.

In 1795, a new actor had appeared on the scene. Napoleon Bonaparte had been gradually coming to the fore, and, in 1796, he assumed the command of the French army in Italy. Until now he had been operating in the North, but in April, having crossed the Po at Piacenza, he defeated the Italian General Beaulieu at Lodi and forced him to fall back on Mantua while he himself entered Milan. Town after town fell to his victorious and rapacious army. Some states endeavoured to placate him, and the Pope had to cede those of his territories which were occupied to the French and to pay a "contribution" in money and works of art. Worse however and more dangerous for Italy were the Jacobin societies which were being formed all over the country, even among the liberal aristocracy. It went so far that the Lombard administration in September 1796 actually announced a competition, "What form of free Government is best fitted to promote the happiness of Italy?"

In 1796 Angelica had so far recovered from her loss that she was painting again in full strength. Her records from now on are a curious mixture, not only do they note her paintings and the sums she received from them as in the past, but they also give the small details of sums given to her young relative, Anton, for such items as a silk dress and some handkerchiefs and little commissions which he executed for her. Her clients were still numerous and varied. One was a Mr. Forbes who commissioned a big picture; he has noted that he had free entry to her studio where she was finishing a picture, "Suffer the little children to come unto Me." This induced him to suggest the subject of "Religion and her lovely train", and Angelica accepted the commission for an enormous canvas, seven feet by nine feet, with life size figures: a formidable task for a woman of her age. When it arrived in England it was unfortunately not greatly admired.

The society feuds of the English colony in Rome passed Angelica by, although she was probably well aware of them. She was more familiar with the circle of artists who clustered around Canova, and in connection with this there is an amusing story of a joke played by the sculptor on his friends.

Canova's friends were in the habit of reading books on art and history to him while he worked so that he might increase his learning. One day they read that a portrait of Giorgione painted by the artist was in Widman's collection. Recollecting a joke played in Venice some few years earlier, Canova decided to play the same prank on the art critics in Rome. He purchased a sixteenth century canvas of a "Holy Family" which he scratched off and painted instead a head of Giorgione, imitating his manner and touch. Prince Rezzonico and Prince d'Este were in the secret, and the former announced at one of the frequent dinners given to artists and men of letters that his nephews, the Widmans, had had the portrait of Giorgione restored and were sending it to Rome to be criticised . . . Finally at a largely attended dinner—amongst the guests being Angelica Kauffmann, Gavin Hamilton, Volpato, Cian Gherardo Rossi, the painter Cavalucci and a certain Burri, a celebrated picture restorer—d'Este came in, breathless and dusty, bearing the precious case, well corded and sealed, under his arm. When the canvas was unpacked, a general chorus went up: Giorgione, Giorgione, very much a Giorgione! The eminent company were in ecstasies over the style, the technique; the effects of light and shade. Burri alone found fault with the restoration of the right eye; but A. Kauffmann opposed him violently and the argument grew hot. Canova entered in the midst of it and was immediately assailed with questions as to his opinion of the picture. The master examined it minutely, then remarked, "It seems to me a good picture, but I understand nothing of painting; had it been a statue I would have ventured an opinion." The discussion became more animated than ever. Gian Gherardo dei Rossi begged the Prince to allow him to have the picture copied by some Portuguese of whose school he was Director—a permission gladly accorded. The copy was sent to Lisbon and the original remained in Prince Rezzonico's possession, who left it to Rossi in memory of the well-conceived joke. It would be interesting to know the feelings of the distinguished company when they learned how they had been so made fun of.

Events were going from bad to worse in Italy; the country staggered from defeat to defeat. Republics were set up following insurrections against the French, and by 18 October the victorious Napoleon concluded a treaty of peace with Austria known as the Treaty of Campoformio. This created the Cisalpine republic but Venice, whose last Doge Ludovico Manin had abdicated, went to Austria. In November of that year Napoleon returned to France. The year 1798 opened disastrously for Rome. On 15 February, a Roman Republic was proclaimed, with Senators, Tribunes and Consuls. Pope Pius VI was deported, first to Tuscany and then to France. Angelica, alone except for her young cousin, was treated with exceptional courtesy by the occupying General de Lespinasse. He left her free from the billeting of troops on her house and in return for this kindness, Angelica painted his portrait. Miss Knight, who with her mother had left the doomed city for Naples, writes in her autobiography that the French general and one of his aides-de-camp forced her to paint their portraits, and carried off from her home all the pictures belonging to Austrians, Russians or English. These were fairly numerous since for some time there had been no means of dispatching them to their respective owners. "I used," wrote Miss Knight, "to send her the news in terms of art, calling the French 'landscape painters' and the English 'historical painters'. Nelson was Don Raphael, but I recollect being puzzled how to inform her that our fleet was gone to Malta, until I thought of referring her for the subject of 'the picture' to a chapter of the *Acts of the Apostles*, well knowing that the book in which that Island was mentioned was not likely to be opened by the inspectors of the post." Miss Knight, like her mother, loathed the French and may have been biased in her report of the depredations in Angelica's house. The French are good judges of art, and although Napoleon carried off the Venetian bronze horses to Paris, it is unlikely that he would burden himself with the work of a contemporary painter when there were so much more precious treasures to be found. In any case, there is no trace of any of Angelica's pictures in their plunder.

It appears that Angelica, nearing the end of her life and deeply moved by all these devastating events, devoted more of her time and thought to painting religious pictures. Clients now came slowly if at all, and there was little to distract her mind from the distressing events around her. She painted a portrait of a Citizen Barass, whom she describes as "a French Count". If this was so, they probably had much to bewail together as she worked. Again she noted, "I have finished the portrait of Citizen (Countess) Thierry, paid for one hundred Zecchini." This entry completes her notes in the M.S. discovered in the Royal Academy Library by Lady Victoria Manners and Dr. G. C. Williamson, which was later deciphered and translated by Donna Stella Vitelleschi.

This MS. is in Italian and it is indispensable as a personal record of the painter's works. At the end of it are the loose leaves which seem to show that Angelica at the end of her life liked to recall some of her most successful paintings and to re-describe them, more for her own satisfaction than for an actual need. She also records sums paid out, and received

from her bankers. It was difficult to get money at this time in
Rome; it was all paper. It was extraordinary indeed that
anyone could travel in such tumultuous days, but curiosity is a
great spur, and though France and England were at war, the
odd traveller still managed to get through. Bonaparte's
brother Joseph had come to Rome as ambassador and
naturally his embassy was the meeting place for every
Jacobin in the city. Pius VI was old, sick and discouraged,
but he hung on to life. The Directory had ordered that, after
his death, no Pope was to be elected. The assassination of
General Duphot did not help matters, for it provided the
Directory with the excuse it needed. General Berthier was
ordered to march on Rome, which he did, and occupied the
city on 10 February 1798. The new Republic was proclaimed a few days later in the historic Forum. Ghastly
events followed; the Pope was assaulted in his own Vatican,
which was plundered, as were the houses of the nobility, the
museums and even the churches. Since the sack of Rome in
the sixteenth century, nothing like it had been seen. One can
imagine in what terror a lonely woman lived, even though
she had her friends around her.

In a letter of October 1799 she spoke of the prospect as
"gloomy beyond expression", and lamented the fact that at a
time of life when she had always expected to enjoy comfort
and release from work, she was forced to labour harder than
ever. This must have been because of the difficulty in getting
funds from abroad or from clients who owed her money. She
said, however, that she was making the best of it and was
resigned to what might yet come.

Robert Dalrymple, who sat to her in 1802, wrote in his
diary of her poor health. This handsome young man seems to
have been one more of her conquests. On 6 March, he called
on her with a letter of introduction from Lord Northwick,
and the diary continues through April and May, till in June
his portrait was finished. He noted the amiability of her
manner and the fact that she spoke English perfectly; he
enjoyed her conversation, and the more he saw of her the
more he esteemed her. On 26 April, the portrait was
finished. "Spent the evening with Angelica Kauffmann. I

like this lady more and more every time I see her. I sat to her for the last time this morning. It is so very strong a likeness that everybody speaks of it. A German addressed me last night at the ball saying that tho' he had never seen me before, he was sure he must have seen my portrait at Angelica Kauffmann's."

In May Angelica fell ill, but this charming individual did not fail in his attention; he called frequently to inquire how she did, and on May he noted that she had had a second fever and was very thin. She seemed much flattered by his calling so frequently to make inquiries. On 5 June came the last visit. "In the evening I called and took leave of Angelica Kauffmann. She is a most amiable and agreeable woman and I have been infinitely happy in her acquaintance. We were mutually sorry to part, the sentiments we entertain towards each other being founded on the sincerest friendship and esteem. She is to finish my portrait as soon as she is able, and to forward it to England by Mr. Hoare. I paid her forty sequins for it (£20) and ten crowns (£5.5) for the frame." The portrait of this ingenuous and charming young officer now hangs in Oxenford Castle, the seat of the Earl of Stair.

Another account of the artist at this time comes from Miss Caroline Wilmot, travelling in the party of the Earl of Mount Cashell, also on a visit to Rome. After a long description of the pleasures and horrors of the city she was taken at last to visit Kauffmann and says, "So much of sculpture have I passed through and so much of admiration have I experienced that if wonder had any petrifying powers I might long have turned into stone. Indeed I did expect this metamorphosis to take place but for a visit I paid to Angelica Kauffmann. I might have remained till Doomsday but for her promethean influence, which animates everything she touches, and tingled me into existence once again. Nor can I think of her without a flash of admiration, independent of the talent which has made her name so celebrated. She allows me to sit with her in the mornings often, as her delicate state of health makes confinement necessary: but her appearance has so much more of mind than body that one forgets that she is more than half way to another world which seems anticipated in her countenance . . . Her delightful mildness of manner and sweetness of voice soothes one like the essence of plaintive music, and the pale transparency of her complexion one attributes less to failing health than to the idea that no other light has ever shone on her but the silver beams of the moon. She speaks when you like of her profession, but it is so secondary an object in one's visit to her house, that we forgot to ask for her pictures till the third time we were in her company. She still continues painting, but slowly, and she seems highly considered among modern artists. One of her pictures of the latest invention is the 'Parting of Coriolanus and his Family' which is extremely beautiful in design as well as in the execution."

Miss Wilmot then goes on to give a particularly vivid account of Angelica's neighbour, the eccentric and magnificent Earl of Bristol, the Lord Bishop of Cloyne and Derry, whom Angelica had painted. This nobleman's splendid mansion housed an equally splendid collection of works of art, and was a meeting place of the artists in Rome, to say nothing of their wives, whose portraits were all over the house. His three favourite mistresses were beautifully represented, says Miss Wilmot, as Juno, Minerva and Venus in the Judgement of Paris. He was an old reprobate, and could be seen driving with one or other of the beauties, and sometimes two together, to the scandal of the neighbourhood. His attire matched his manners; on his head he wore a purple nightcap, with a tassel of gold dangling over his shoulder, and a sort of mitre in front; silk stockings and slippers of the same colour, and a short round petticoat such as Bishops wear, fringed with gold about his knees. A loose dressing gown of silk was thrown around his shoulders. In this Merry Andrew trim he rode on horseback, to the never-ending amazement of all beholders. But Miss Wilmot does him the justice to record that he admired the Arts, supported the Artists, and spent such a quantity of money in Italy "that among other rarities he has purchased, he has also purchased Friends". As a proof of his eminence in criticism of the fine arts, we may cite the episode quoted by Memes in his life of Canova. The Earl had ventured to find some fault with the sculpture of the group of Theseus and the Minotaur saying that it was "too cold" but, at the same time, bestowing just commendation on the simplicity and purity of the style, and recommending the sculptor to preserve the same manner in another similar performance, devoted to a more impassioned subject. To this Canova listened in silence. But in a short time he produced the model of that most lovely work, his well-known *Cupid and Psyche*. To his lordship's expressions of surprise and pleasure the unassuming artist merely replied, "I always prefer to answer a judicious observation with my chisel rather than with words."

Canova was at this time a close friend of our Angelica. He had retired to the country, to his native village, horrified at the depredations of the occupying French in stripping Rome of its treasures, and when he returned, it was with his great *Perseus* which was placed in the vacancy created by the loss of the *Apollo Belvedere*. The two creative artists must have mourned together, but felt that in spite of the difficulties of living, for them Rome remained the classic centre of the art world. Angelica's main occupation at this time was the painting of her last religious picture. It was for the church of her father's birthplace, the village of Schwarzenberg, and represented the Blessed Virgin crowned by the three Persons of the Trinity. She was able to complete it and have it conveyed to Schwarzenberg where it hangs today. But when she started her "Coriolanus" and another oval of a young girl who had sat down to rest while gathering flowers and fallen asleep, it was too much for her, and she contracted another chill, which developed into pneumonia. When she had recovered, her physicians recommended her to leave Rome for a time at least.

So with her faithful cousin Anton, she went to Florence and Bologna, and thence to Como, where she had not been since she was a child. Here her cousin left her, going to Bregenz to visit his relations there, while Angelica remained, much restored in mind and body, and able to enjoy the remembered beauty of the lake and the countryside. From here she wrote a letter to a friend telling in very allegorical language of an experience which hints at a last late flowering of love. "It was here in my youth that I tasted my first pleasures. I saw rich palaces and carriages, fine ships and a splendid theatre. It seemed to me a Paradise. I also saw Cupid in the act of shooting his arrow at my breast. Still a child, I escaped, and the dart passed me by. Long afterwards I came back to these pleasant parts. I enjoyed the pleasures of ripe age, friends and the beauty of the lake. Walking one day with pleasant companions, I saw Cupid sleeping in a shady wood. He awoke and greeted me. He recognised me in spite of my silver hairs. He leaped up quickly to avenge himself, threw his dart and very nearly struck me." Angelica's biographers have all regarded this episode as cryptic. We know from a later letter to Captain Robert Dalrymple that they had met again unexpectedly in Como, and in the letter she assures him that she will never forget the happy hours spent in his society. May we not infer that Angelica was in love, to her own surprise perhaps, in love with this handsome sensitive young man, with whom she had spent so much time in Rome. The last movement of a starved heart, which she recognised from the first as quite impossible. For she had enjoyed everything in her life, fame, wealth, admiration, affection, but that which women hold most precious she had missed, a satisfying, fully realised love. Alas for her, birth, rank, and above all, age separated them, and it is probable that the young officer never even guessed what was passing in his friend's mind.

From Como she went to Venice where she spent some days with her husband's family, and then she travelled slowly back to her beloved Rome, reliving for the last time her past, and received everywhere with the respect due to her fame and her ageless charm. On reaching Rome she was greeted with an account of the reception of her picture in Schwartzenberg. It had been arranged that the picture should be shown to the people on St. Michael's day, and crowds had come for the occasion. The whole village and the vicinity were en fete, and the church could not hold them all, large as it was. So an altar was erected in the piazza outside, where Mass was celebrated, and at the end of the day the picture was carried in procession to its place

Dr. John Morgan. Courtesy of the Washington County Historical Society.

in the Church. Angelica's pleasure was shared by her Roman friends, who gave a fête in her honour; verses were dedicated to her, and with song and much wine and merry-making, her triumph was complete.

Renewed health brought renewed impetus to work; she set to with fresh zest, clients came, among them the King and Queen of Sardinia, and Canova, faithful as ever, even asked her to sketch some figures of Cupid which he executed in marble for a frieze. But it was impossible to ignore the growing disturbance, both in Italy where Napoleon's successes were at their height, or abroad, where war was the chief preoccupation. It was impossible to count on remittances from England, or indeed from anywhere else, and a letter at this time—1805—to Captain Dalrymple gives an idea of her state of mind. This is the letter with the clue to their having met since his departure from Rome.

"Rome April the 19th, 1805.
Much honoured friend,
Vain is the attempt to express the joy with which I read your kind and obliging letter date Feb. 24. The agreeable surprise at the sight of it can only be compared to that when unexpected I had the happiness to see you at Como. Accept then my sincerest thanks for your kind remembrance of me, and be assured that I shall never forget the happy hours spent in your society. The same impression I am certain remains in the heart of everyone that has had the satisfaction to know you and to converse with you. Your letter is dated from Chatham which place I have seen when I left England on my way to Margate where I embarked for Ostend ... I dare say that your journey to Scotland was pleasant and all your friends must have seen you with joy, especially your worthy father—but I can well suppose the pains of parting, but what else is our life but a mixture of joy and sorrow, of the latter perhaps the greater dose. I am much obliged to you my worthy friend, for the kind interest you take concerning my health. Thank God I am perfectly well

and have been so all this winter past, have also been much occupied with historical pictures and portraits. We have had some travellers this winter of Northern nations but few English except the Duchess of Cumberland and the Mountcashell and Cloncurry family who I believe are preparing for their departure. We expect the return of the Holy Father next month."

This letter shows the pleasure she has in chatting with her friend and what importance she attached to renewed connection with those of her patrons she most valued. She goes on to say how much she wished to be able to entertain him with news about the fine arts in Rome. The excavations at Ostia are to be continued as also those which the Queen of Naples has made at Pompeii. The Arch of Septimus has been entirely uncovered and the same will be done with the Arch of Constantine. She describes the fine works of Canova and the statue which he has made of Napoleon and the mother of the Emperor, and finally of the statue of the Princess Pauline Borghese. And last she alludes to the work of someone whom she calls Zoowals, a Dane who must be Thorwaldsen, for his "Jason" was finished about then and was much admired by Canova.

She concludes by telling him of the death of the Bishop of Derry, all of whose stupendous collection is to be sold, and emphasises what a loss his death will be for many artists, especially in the present hard times.

In the year following she was again able to leave Rome for a visit to Albano, and from there she wrote a letter to Mr. Bowles of Wanstead in which she tells him of her restored health and mentions a picture to be sent to him. She thanks him for all his kindness and expresses her sincere attachment. Her generous nature shows again and again in her personal attachment to her clients to whom she constantly insisted on making gifts of pictures for which they would very willingly have paid.

Shortly after her return to Rome she fell ill again. She was failing fast, but when she could take her usual drive through the streets of Rome the people greeted her as a

familiar and loved friend, and still every traveller who came
to the city wished to be presented to her. Her last pictures
were of the young daughter of the Duke and Duchess of
Miranda and a Magdalene which she executed for the
Count Pezzoli of Bergamo, a small but lovely picture with
all her lightness of touch and brilliance of colouring.

She made then a short visit to Tivoli. All these places
must in her present mood have recalled the happy times she
had passed there in company with her most valued friends;
here Goethe had sat and drawn its beauties, here Herder
had read his poems, here her beloved father had been with
her, and here she had lived the days of her exuberant youth,
with Hamilton, yes, and Nathaniel Dance, and even Fuseli
who had so passionately loved her. She wrote to her old
friend Mr. Forbes:

"My kindest and warmest thanks have this time been
longer delayed on account of a little excursion made into
the country. I passed near three weeks at Tivoli, about
twenty miles from Rome, a charming place so much sung
and praised by Horace, where he had his villa, of which,
however, little or nothing remains. More is yet to be seen
of the villa of Maecenas and the villa Adriana and others,
but destructive Time has reduced all to the pleasures of
imagination—perhaps a melancholy pleasure, to see only
poor remains of the greatest magnificence. Oh, that you
my friend could see this place or that I could once more
have the happiness to see you in dear England, to which
my heart is so attached, and where I should once more
see you, my worthy friend, with the greatest joy. Too
happy should I be to be myself the bearer of the picture I
had the pleasure of executing for you. In Peaceable times
it would not perhaps have been among the impossible
things: could I however find in the meantime a safe
opportunity of getting it conveyed to you, I shall certainly not lose it, as I long that you should at least have
this token of my gratitude for the many and numberless
obligations, for all the favours which you continue to
bestow upon me. It makes me very happy that you and all

your family are well. Be so kind as to remember me to them in the most respectful manner. I beg for the continuance of your friendship, and have the honour to be with the greatest esteem and gratitude

Your most humble and obliged servant and friend

Angelica Kauffmann."

When shorn of the obligatory rhetoric of the time, these letters show most clearly the relationship which Angelica had with many of her patrons. Not only did she paint them, she established a sympathy, a close harmony with them and it was this which made it possible for her to make such a "speaking likeness" of most of her sitters.

We have no other evidence of the last months of her life. She continued her accustomed round as long as she was able, slowly fading a little day by day. She occupied herself in going through her papers and destroying the greater part of them. She knew and accepted that she was spending her last remaining days, comforted by the love of her friends and the certitude that she had in her faith. She was attended with the greatest devotion by her cousin and he was with her when she passed peacefully away on the 5th of November 1807. Two days later, Bonomi received a letter from a correspondent in Rome, a Mr. M. A. Rossi in which the latter told him:

"... What for some time I foresaw, after twenty days of confinement in bed, with the greatest tranquillity of spirit, always present to her self, having twice received the Blessed Sacrament, and, two days before, Extreme Unction, perfectly resigned, courageously she met the death of the righteous: Thursday last 5th inst. at half past two in the afternoon, the great woman, the always holy, illustrious, and most pious, Angelica Kauffmann. I shudder in acquainting you with such unfortunate news, knowing the grief it will cause to you and Mrs. Bonomi. I shall now relate the particulars of her illness and funeral. During her severe illness, all her numerous friends did what they could to restore her, and everyone was grieved in apprehension of losing her: you may

easily believe more than I can express, how much their
grief increased at her death. I only therefore shall mention that they vied with each other in endeavouring to
perform their last duties in the most decorous obsequies,
celebrated this morning in the church of San Andrea delle
Fratte, conducted by Canova and other *virtuosi* friends.
The church was decorated as is customary for nobles.
At ten o'clock in the morning the corpse was accompanied to the church by two very numerous brother-
hoods, fifty capuchins and fifty priests. The bier was
carried by some of the brotherhood, but the four corners
of the pall by four young ladies properly dressed for the
occasion; the four tassels were held by the four first
gentlemen of the Academy; these were followed by the
rest of the Academicians and virtuosi who carried in
triumph two of her pictures, and every one with large
wax tapers lighted.

This is the melancholy account I thought it my duty
to transmit to you. I shall take the first opportunity of
communicating to you any further intelligence I may
receive on this subject."

Bonomi passed this letter on to the Royal Academy and
it was read at their General Assembly on 23 December
when they registered the death of their esteemed colleague.
Whether they regretted it suitably is not mentioned in the
note which Farington made; it is a bare statement of the
fact. But in Rome things were different. There she had
lived and been known and loved; the church where she was
to be buried was not far from her dwelling. Here she had
walked and been seen by all the neighbours as she went to
her daily Mass, they had felt honoured by her reception of
the crowned heads and all the other royal and noble sitters
who had come to her studio. So, when all the notabilities
gathered to do her honour, it is certain that every window
and doorway was filled with the ordinary people of her
quarter who mourned her loss with them. The arrangements, quickly organised, were of the most splendid character. The church of San Andrea delle Fratte was filled with

the most eminent citizens of Rome, who walked in procession to it, and were received by her cousin Anton, by Canova and by her two especial friends, the architect Uggieri and the sculptor Carlo Albacini. All the members of the Accademia di San Luca, of which she had also been a member, were there, and representatives from many Academies all over Italy and from France and Portugal made up the train. And we are informed that it was one of the longest processions ever seen in the city, only equalled by that of Raphael. Two of her best religious pictures, as Rossi had related, were carried into the church and placed on either side of the altar, and a bust of herself executed by Canova only a month before she died was placed near them. It was her special wish that she should lie beside her husband, and her body was interred in the third small chapel on the right of the church, but later Zucchi's body was removed by order of her executors, who realised that she had meant in the very place where he had lain, and that is where it now rests, above it the handsome monument bearing the following inscription in Latin:

Antonio Pietro Son of Francesco Zucchi
A Venetian. For the love of God and of the poor
and for fame in Painting
Here lies entombed.
He lived 69 years 7 months 26 days and died on the
26 of May
In the year of the World's Redemption 1795
Angelica Kauffmann
To tears and sorrow condemned for a husband
Most sweet and most benign
Even against his own wish, has dedicated this monument.
Also here lies buried Angelica Daughter of Joseph Johann
Kauffmann
Of a Schwarzenberg family
Of the greatest renown in painting
Who merited a cenotaph in the church of the Pantheon
But she herself in this tomb
Which she had erected to Antonio Zucchi

Gave orders to be interred
So that with a husband who was most congenial to her
She might after sepulture also dwell
She was aged 66 years and 6 days
She died in Rome the 5th of November 1807
Hail! Most excellent woman, and dwell in peace.

Angelica's bust was duly set up in the Pantheon with great ceremonial and a similar marble bust was sent to Schwarzenberg, where it may be seen in the Church. Beneath it is an inscription with the following verse:

Sie war als Mensch, als Christ, als Kunstler gross auf Erden
Willst Du, hier und dort Dir und andern nutzlich werden
Wie sie Ehre, Ruhm erzwingen haben
Schätze Tugend, benutz Talente des Schöpfers Gaben

which may be translated "Oh earth she was great as human being, as Christian and as artist, wouldst thou be useful to thyself and others, and like her conquer honour and fame, then do as she did, prize virtue, use talent, both gifts of the Creator".

Anton Johann Kauffmann would write to Madame Bonomi. "These days is celebrated the anniversary of our cousin Angelica in the Rotonda (The Pantheon) and her bust will be presented ... A magnificent Requiem has been made with about two hundred Holy Masses in suffrage of her soul, besides many other things performed in her honour, so that since the death of Raphael of Urbino till now a similar funeral has not been made in Rome."

Angelica left a very long will in which she thanked her servants who had been with her for years and left them handsome presents. She spoke of her "beloved" husband and sent all the silver bearing his initials to his relations in Venice. And with it the engravings and drawings which he had left to her, together with books, a table clock made by the Royal clockmaker and many other interesting articles including jewellery. She left the rest of her belongings, as was proper, to Kauffmanns; all the cousins, nieces, etc., were remembered and she had done her best to partition her money among them. None was left out, and her own collection of paintings and works of art were to be sold and the proceeds given to the poor of the district when her relations were provided for. It was an exemplary testament.

So this great woman died, as she had lived, practical and full of common sense, but with a noble integrity, having served her God, her Art, and her friends with every breath she drew.

In an age like our own, which has seen the formal abandonment of Greek and Latin as the two cornerstones of a good education, and which has shifted away from literary values, classical or otherwise in favour of scientific studies, it is difficult to imagine the impact of a painting with a mythical or historical theme upon an audience steeped in recollections of the Greek or Roman past. To them the names of Hecuba, Achilles, Ulysses, Venus, Aeneas or even Penelope were as familiar as those of their own rulers or politicians. Even the two classical painters whom Ruskin recognised, Poussin and Claude, have only in the past forty years enjoyed a belated recognition. If his main contention is right, and the neo-classicists were handicapped by their unbelief since "Labour must be banished because it was to be unrewarded, humiliation of body must be prevented since there could be no compensation for them by preparation of the soul for another world", this does not hold good for Angelica, a devout Catholic. But it is significant that she only painted four religious pictures. She said that it was because it was difficult for her to depict God or the Holy Family, but it may very well have been because she had few clients who asked for such subjects. And those she produced never achieved the force of her best classical designs, or even the spontaneous charm—reminiscent of Boucher—of the "Girl with Flowers".

We must remember that as a woman she had to be successful or, like her friend Mary Moser, be completely forgotten. And for this reason alone she had to pay attention to the taste of the society she lived in during her London period. But she brought with her from Rome all that she had learned there, and in London she had the honour, with Benjamin West, of introducing the neo-classical period, and here she painted some of her best pictures in that genre. With her return to Rome she came under the influence of Mengs, and Batoni, and when one places her pictures in sharp relation to such masters, apart from superficial likeness, in the handling of drapery or grouping, in sheer handling of the material of painting, she survives the comparison. Added to this are her womanly grace, her sensitive feeling for colour, and instinctive understanding of her subjects.

It is true that she repeated her own compositions frequently, as they did, but the new mastery which developed in the latter period of her life is apparent in the big Bariatinsky group, in the self portrait in the Uffizi, and particularly in the lovely "Lady Hamilton as the Muse of Comedy". In conclusion I may quote the eminent author of an article which was printed in the Catalogue of the great exhibition in Bregenz in 1968, Mr. Anthony Clark. "I strongly believe that Angelica was a first-rate painter, and indeed, occupied a position of the first rank. Her quality and her position have nothing to do with her sex. Her Age thought that she far out-distanced normal possibilities as a woman, but was particularly fascinated by the fact that she WAS a woman as well as a great artist. The understanding of greatness in her Age was different from ours, but I believe that Angelica Kauffmann's best paintings are of a lasting greatness and value."

BIBLIOGRAPHY

Acton, Harold, *The Bourbons of Naples*, Methuen and Co.
Apollo Magazine, July-December 1963.
Bariatinski, Prince *My Russian Life*.
Brissot, Jean Pierre de Warville, *Memoires*.
Beckford, W. *The Life and Letters*.
Burton, Elizabeth, *The Georgians at Home*, Longmans 1907.
Busiri Vici, Andrea, *Apollo*, January-June 1963.
Clarke, Mrs Godfrey, *Gleanings from an old Portfolio*, 1898.
Crawford, Marion, *Gleanings from Venetian History*, Macmillan 1907.
The Connoisseur, September 1946.
The Connoisseur, July-December 1947.
The Connoisseur, September 1965.
Delany, Mrs, *A Memoir*, George Paston. Grant Richards 1909.
Fothergill, Brian, *Sir William Hamilton*, Faber.
Farington, Joseph, *Diaries*.
Gerard, Frances A., *Angelika Kauffmann*, London 1892.
Goethe, *Zur nachgeschite der Italinische Reise. Goethe's briefwechsel mit Freunden und Kunstgenossen in Italien 1788-1790*. Schriften der Goethe Gesellschaft.
Harnack, Otto, *Goethe's Breif Wechsel Mit freunden*, Weimar 1892.
Hardy, *Memoirs of the Earl of Charlemont*, 1810.
Hartcup, Adeline, *Angelica Kauffmann*, Heinemann.
Honour, Hugh, *The New Classicism*.
Knight, Cornelia, *Autobiography*, Allen and Co, London 1861.
Knowles, John, F.R.S., *The Life and Writings of Henry Fuseli*, London 1831.
Knight, *Lady Knight's Letters from France and Italy*, Arthur Humphreys 1905.
Keate, George, *Epistle to Angelica Kauffmann*.
Lennox, Lady Sarah, *Life and Letters*.
Mahon, Denis, *The Catalogue of the Guercino Exhibition*, Bologna 1968.
Manners and Williamson, *Angelica Kauffmann*, The Bodley Head.
Memes, J. S., *Memoirs of Antonio Canova*, Edinburgh 1825.
Melvill, Lewis, *The Berry Papers*, John Lane 1914.
Maxwell, Conatantia, *Dublin under the Georges*, Faber.
Paston, George, *Lady Wortley Montague*, Methuen 1907.
——, *Sidelights on the Georgian Period*, Methuen 1902.
Pater, Walter, *The Renaissance*, (essay on Winckelmann), Macmillan.
Piozzi, Hester, *Journey through France and Italy and Germany*.
——, *Anecdotes of the late Samuel Johnson*, 4th Edition, Printed for Cadell in the Strand.
——, *The Postchaise Companion or Travellers Directory through Ireland*, 1750.
Ruskin, John, *Stones of Venice*, Smith Elder and Co 1853.
Rossi, G. G., *Vita di Angelica Kauffmann*, tr German by Alois Weinhart, Breqenz 1814.
Salvatorelli, *A concise History of Italy*, Allen and Unwin.
Smith, J. T., *Antiquities of London*.
——, *Nollekens and his Times*, John Lane, The Bodley Head.
Schreiber, Lady Charlotte, *Fans and Fan Leaves*.
Timbs, John, F.S.A., *Anecdotal Biography*, London 1860.
Wilmot, Catherine, *An Irish Peer on the Continent*, Williams and Norgate.
Walpole, Horace, *Letters*, Richard Bentley and Son 1891.
Walcot, Dr, *Peter Pindar's Odes to Royal Academicians*, 1782.
Whitley Papers, Victoria and Albert Museum, Dept. of Prints and Drawings.
Winckelmann, J. J., *History of Ancient Art among the Greeks*, tr John Lodge, 1850.

INDEX